Twayne's English Authors Series

Sylvia E. Bowman, *Editor*

INDIANA UNIVERSITY

Sir John Davies

TEAS 175

Sir John Davies

By JAMES L. SANDERSON

Rutgers University

TWAYNE PUBLISHERS
A DIVISION OF G. K. HALL & CO., BOSTON

Library of Congress Cataloging in Publication Data

Sanderson, James L.
    Sir John Davies.

    (Twayne's English authors series; TEAS 175)
    Bibliography: pp. 159–63.
    Includes index.
    1. Davies, Sir John, 1569–1626.
PR2242.D2S2   821'.3   74-20817
ISBN 0–8057–1141–1

PR
2242
.D2S2

To

Scott and Stuart

Contents

About the Author

James L. Sanderson is Professor of English at Rutgers University Camden College of Arts and Sciences, where he has taught since 1960 and has served for a number of years as chairman of the English Department. He holds A.B. and M.A. degrees from the University of Michigan and the Ph.D. from the University of Pennsylvania. The editor of Shakespeare's *Henry the Fourth, Part One* for the Norton Critical Editions Series, he is a co-editor of *Exposition and the English Language* and three drama anthologies. Professor Sanderson's principal areas of scholarly interest are Shakespeare and English prose and poetry of the sixteenth and seventeenth centuries, and his work has appeared in *American Speech, English Journal, English Language Notes, English Literary Renaissance, The Library, The Library Chronicle, Modern Language Review, Review of English Studies,* and *Texas Studies in Language and Literature.* He is a recipient of a Rutgers University Faculty Research Fellowship and an American Philosophical Society Travel Grant, which made it possible for him to pursue the research required for the present volume at the Bodleian Library, the British Museum, and the Huntington Library.

Preface

Sir John Davies (1569–1626) was a man of many, diverse, and distinguished talents; indeed, he was an example of the "compleat" gentleman often envisioned by writers of Renaissance courtesy books. Well read in Classical and in his native literature, Davies was a student of the theory and practice of law; of legal, political, and social history; of philosophy and theology; and of civil administration. A graceful poet and serious scholar, he was highly adept in practical affairs; and he efficiently discharged the duties of demanding governmental positions in Ireland. His combination of boundless energy, intellectual ability, and great practical competence places him among those zesty, assertive, colorful, and able Englishmen whose actions, whether in geographic exploration or in intellectual inquiry, in political or in economic enterprise, in the New World or at home, did so much to propel England into the Modern Era.

But it is with Davies' work as a poet that this volume is principally concerned. Although his poetry has not been neglected by scholars and critics, much of the published commentary has been either bibliographical or limited in focus to one poem or another. The results of immense scholarly energies embodied in doctoral dissertations have not received very wide dissemination. Except for Margarete Seemann's monograph in German, no comprehensive critical account of Davies' poetry has been published—a need that this book seeks to fill.

Following a chapter treating Davies' life and the influences on him as a writer, attention is directed to his poems as expressions of the period in which they were written and as works of continuing literary interest. This study proposes no really drastic change in the traditional assessments of Davies' poetry, but it does confirm the approbation which the poet has received and attempts to facilitate the modern reader's enjoyment and understanding of the poems.

The notes reflect my considerable debt to other students of Davies' poetry. But I should like here especially to thank the Reverend T. C. Childs and Professor Robert Krueger for sharing their knowledge of Davies with me and for permitting me to consult their theses concerning Davies which are now in the Bodleian Library. Unfortunately, Dr. Krueger's fine edition of Davies' poems, published in 1974 by The Clarendon Press, appeared too late to be used in this study. I wish also to express my appreciation to my colleague Professor Sheema Z. Buehne, who read the manuscript with care and insight and made a number of suggestions in behalf of clarity and English grammar. A grant from the Penrose Fund awarded by the American Philosophical Society permitted me to travel to distant libraries, and a Faculty Fellowship awarded by The Research Council of Rutgers University afforded me the leisure required to complete this study. To my wife, Rosamond, I owe a debt which passeth all understanding but lacketh not appreciation.

JAMES L. SANDERSON

Camden, New Jersey

Acknowledgment

I wish to thank the Keeper of Western Manuscripts of the Bodleian Library for permission to quote from manuscripts belonging to the Bodleian Library, Oxford.

Chronology

1569   John Davies born at Chisgrove, Wiltshire, son of John and Mary.

1570   Death of the poet's father.

1580   Matriculated at Winchester College.

1585   Matriculated at Queens College, Oxford.

1587–   Admitted to Middle Temple, London.
1588

1590   Death of poet's mother.

1592   Travel to Continent; visit with Paul Merula, Dutch scholar and jurist.

1594   *Orchestra* entered in *Stationers' Register*.

1595   Called to the Bar.

ca. 1595   Wrote "Epithalamion"; *Epigrams* published.

1596   *Orchestra* published.

ca. 1597   Wrote "Gulling Sonnets."

1597–   Attack on Richard Martin; expulsion from Middle
1598   Temple and disbarment.

1599   Published *Nosce Teipsum* and *Hymnes of Astraea*.

ca. 1600   Attended meetings of Society of Antiquaries.

1601   Petition for re-admission to Middle Temple granted. Elected Member of Parliament for Corfe Castle, Dorsetshire.

1602   *Ten Sonnets to Philomel* published in *A Poetical Rhapsody*.

1603   Traveled to Scotland with party to welcome James I. Appointed Solicitor-General for Ireland; proceeded to Dublin in November to assume office. Knighted.

1606   Appointed Attorney-General for Ireland and Serjeant-at-Law.

1608   *Yet Other Twelve Wonders of the World*, *A Lotterie*, and *A Contention betwixt a Wife, a Widdowe and a Maide* published in *A Poetical Rhapsody*.

1609   Married Eleanor Touchet, daughter of George, Baron Audley.

1612   Published *A Discovery of True Causes.* Elected Member of Parliament for Fermanagh, Ireland.

1613   Elected Speaker of the Lower House of Irish Parliament.

1615   Published *Le Primer Report des Cases et Matters en Ley.*

1619   Recalled to England; resumed professional practice as King's Serjeant and served as circuit judge.

1621   Elected Member of Parliament for Newcastle-under-Lyne.

1622   Collected edition of *Orchestra, Hymnes of Astraea,* and *Nosce Teipsum* published.

ca. 1624   Wrote "Metaphrase" of Psalms 1–50.

1626   Appointed Lord Chief Justice in November. Died unexpectedly December 7, 1626, before taking office.

CHAPTER 1

Sweet Poet and Grave Lawyer

POET, jurist, scholar, civil servant, Sir John Davies was a man of many accomplishments and distinctions; and the details of his life have been written many times. While we lack information concerning his early youth and student days, there is substantial agreement about the principal configurations of his career. His life falls into four phases: education and preparation for a career; professional setback and ostracism; recovery of his prospects and long service to the British crown in Ireland; and return to England to enjoy his fortune and to be named Chief Justice.[1]

I Years of Study

Davies was born at Chisgrove (or Chicksgrove) in the hamlet of Tysbury, Wiltshire, where the parish register records his baptism on April 16, 1569. His mother, Mary, was the daughter of John Bennett of Pitt House, Wiltshire, and a member of a family of some prominence in the county.[2] His father, John, of Welsh descent, has been described by John Aubrey and Anthony à Wood as a "wealthy tanner";[3] but this description has been challenged by A. B. Grosart.[4] Whatever his social status, the elder Davies was sufficiently prosperous to assure good educations for two of his sons, Matthew and John. The poet's father died in 1570, however, leaving the rearing and education of the children to his wife, who lived until 1590.

The earliest information concerning Davies' formal education is his admission in 1580 to Winchester College at the age of eleven.[5] As preparation for the rigorous work at Winchester, the young Davies, from either his local petty school or private tutelage, probably had learned to read and write and had,

15

perhaps, been introduced to Latin. Winchester College, one of
the better grammar schools of the day, had been founded in
1387 by William of Wykeham, bishop of Winchester, who had
envisioned it as a school where students might learn that
"grammar [which] is the foundation, gate and source of all the
liberal arts, without which such arts cannot be known, nor
can anyone arrive at practising them."[6] By "grammar" was
meant Latin grammar and literature, although Greek and
Hebrew were sometimes part of the curriculum at such schools.
But the principal work was instruction in Latin; and the
energies, both intellectual and physical, of the teachers were
directed toward drilling, and not infrequently beating, the
elements of Latin grammar and good Latin prose style into
their students.[7]

Such a program demanded hard days of work by the students,
a regimen which would strike us today with our notions of
child-oriented curricula and nondirective approaches to ele-
mentary education as grim indeed. Roused at five in the morning,
the boys had completed three hours of class work before they
paused for breakfast. By bedtime, shortly after eight in the
evening, they would have spent ten hours either in, or preparing
for, class, broken by fairly short intervals for four meals and
some allowance for a limited amount of free time toward
evening. These hours were spent in memorizing declensions and
conjugations, absorbing vocabulary, translating Latin texts into
English and English into Latin, writing Latin prose and poetry,
declaiming, debating, and occasionally acting plays in Latin.[8]

But the mastery of Latin had a purpose besides the mental
discipline which its study was believed to provide. As Wykeham
had said, it was also a "gate" to the wisdom and learning
preserved in the great literary works of Classical times, works
which were so venerated in the Renaissance. The impressive
list of authors read at Winchester included Ovid, Virgil, Salust,
Cicero, Terence, Horace, Martial, Aesop, and Lucian, as well
as some neo-Latin authors like Erasmus and Buchanan. During
these years young Davies must have absorbed much of the
Classical literature which colored his later writing and adorned
his discourse. The prominence given at Winchester to the
reading and imitation of Martial is particularly interesting; for

three of Davies' fellow-students—John Hoskins, Thomas Bastard, and John Owen—were later noted for their volumes of epigrams. And among Davies' earliest poetic efforts in London were satiric epigrams, for which he came to be known as the "English Martial."

After Winchester, Davies proceeded to Oxford University, where he was admitted on October 15, 1585.[9] Although in some ways his life at the university would be similar to that at Winchester, there were important differences; and he probably experienced the exhilaration of most young men who move into the larger and more adult world of university life. Oxford University was a large corporate entity presided over by administrative officers, but its principal components were the individual and largely autonomous colleges, each with its own living quarters, dining hall, chapel, library, faculty, and administrative head.[10] The student's instructional, intellectual, and social life centered in his college where he lived and studied. Although the colleges seem to have been paternalistic toward their students and although physical punishment was on occasion meted out to them, discipline and supervision were probably less rigid and pervasive than in the grammar schools.

The undergraduate program was based on the Latin which the students were expected to have mastered in the grammar schools. During their first two years, the students studied the rhetoric and logic of Aristotle, supplemented with arithmetic and music. In the second year, they were introduced to an academic exercise known as "disputations," debates by their senior students in which the participants attempted to display in Latin their general knowledge, oratorical skills, command of logic, and keen perception of the inadequacies and illogicalities of their opponents' arguments. Having observed such debates, the students devoted much of their third and fourth years in actual debate. Rounding out the undergraduate work were lectures, tutorial studies, and the independent reading which sometimes accounts for much of a college student's education. There seems to be no reason to challenge Wood's statement that Davies "laid a considerable foundation of academical literature, partly by his own natural parts (which were excellent) and partly by the help of a good tutor."[11]

There exist, however, some uncertainties about Davies' career
at Oxford. Among the Carte manuscripts at the Bodleian Library
is a brief, and sometimes inaccurate, biographical account
(MS. Carte 62, ff. 590-1) headed "Notes of the Life of Sr John
Dauys. May 2^d 1674" (hereafter cited as "Carte Notes"). This
document claims that Davies matriculated at New College,
Oxford, an institution also founded by William of Wykeham for
which the bishop seems to have intended Winchester College
as a preparatory school. Davies' own brother Matthew,[12] as did
many Wykehamites, proceeded to New College from Winchester. But the university records list the poet not as a member
of New College but of Queen's College. There is also some
question as to whether Davies ever took his degree. Anthony
à Wood lists him in his *Fasti Oxonienses* as taking the
Bachelor of Arts on July 9, 1590;[13] but the university records
identify this Davies as proceeding to his degree from Magdalen
College.[14] While it was not impossible for students to matriculate
at one college and graduate from another, that our poet did so
is uncertain, for there was yet another "John Davies" at the
university who had matriculated in 1585 at Magdalen and who
might be the Davies listed by Wood.

The poet's admission to the Middle Temple in 1587 suggests
the possibility that Davies did not take a degree at all, which
was not necessarily an exceptional practice. Not all of the
students at the university directed their work toward degrees;
in fact, spending a year or so at one of the universities as a
bridge between grammar school and the Inns of Court or
simply as a diversional period for a gentleman-to-be was becoming fashionable in the education of young men of means.[15]
Those who, in the words of the "Carte Notes," had "designed
[Davies] for a lawyer," might have viewed such a plan for
one "Not being tried and tutor'd in the world" as an opportunity
for the youth to gain greater maturity before proceeding to the
Middle Temple—and the myriad distractions and extra-scholastic
allures of London.

Davies' admission to the Middle Temple, where, as he was
to say years later, he had his "chiefest education," is recorded as
follows: "10 Feb., 1587. Mr. John, third son of John Davis of
Tisburie, Wilts, gent., and late of New Inn, gent., generally;

fine, 20s. Bound with Messrs. Lewes and Raynoldes."[16] On the basis of this entry, A. B. Grosart and others have argued that Davies' father had been associated with New Inn and was a legal practitioner. But, having more carefully studied the entry forms in the Middle Temple records, more recent scholars have insisted that the phrase "late of New Inn, gent." should be construed in apposition with "Mr. John," thereby indicating that, prior to his admission to the Middle Temple, the *poet* had spent a period in New Inn.[17] Such a pattern would have been quite a normal one, for New Inn was one of several "Inns of Chancery," which, according to John Stowe, served both as living quarters for various officers connected with the courts and as places for the instruction of young students in "the first elements and grounds of the lawe."[18]

The Middle Temple was one of the four Inns of Court in London, the main sources of instruction and training in the common law. The other three Inns were Lincoln's Inn, Gray's Inn, and the Inner Temple. Each Inn was an independent institution and, besides providing legal instruction, furnished its members with chambers, a dining hall, a chapel, and a corporate social life. In many ways, the Inns were similar to the colleges at Oxford and Cambridge; and they, along with their related Inns of Chancery, constituted, as Sir Edward Coke observed, "the most famous university for profession of the law only, or any one humane science, that is in the world."[19]

As more and better books became available, law students increasingly began to "read law"; but, when Davies was at the Middle Temple, an important part of the legal training was still gained through various oral exercises. These included "bolts," arguments on legal cases and questions before a court of the faculty; "moots," public disputations by senior members of the Inn; and "readings," formal expositions of selected statutes. These "readings" were delivered twice each year by distinguished senior lawyers and constituted a major element of the students' education. The proximity of the Inns to the law courts gave the students opportunities to observe firsthand court procedures and techniques.[20]

The study required to qualify one to practice law was long. Usually some seven to eight years were necessary before a student was called to the bar and thereby designated "Utter Barrister." Three more years of work qualified him to practice law in all of the courts. The distinction of "Bencher," meaning one regarded as qualified to offer one of the Readings, followed only after ten to twelve years of practice as an Utter Barrister. Not all of the residents at the Inns, however, envisioned completing such programs; many of the students sought primarily to equip themselves to manage landed estates or to protect their business interests in an age famous for its ready resort to litigation. Others studied law as an appropriate preparation for governmental careers or service to some nobleman. For still others, the Inns served as finishing schools where they might "obtain the social cachet so avidly sought by the rising gentry of the Elizabethan period"[21] in the scramble for favor and preferment in a courtly society. A number of older lawyers, too, retained their quarters at their Inns for their convenience when coming to London during the court sessions. The residents Davies encountered at the Inns were, therefore, men with varied talents and purposes and included some of the most brilliant figures of the times. Aside from the Court itself, they constituted "the liveliest, the most intelligent, and certainly the most influential society England could furnish."[22]

The study of law was enlivened—sometimes totally disrupted— by the lavish celebrations at Christmastime and by the entertainments which the affluent Readers were expected to provide during their terms of office. Feasts, dances, masques, receptions for important persons (including the monarch), and Saturnalian frolics brightly colored the life at the Inns. The law students were also noted for their literary interests, both as writers and as readers. A long list of familiar English authors could be compiled from the registers at the Inns. John Donne, John Marston, Benjamin Rudyard, and John Hoskins were among Davies' contemporary law students; and one can imagine how such talents could stimulate a young poet like Davies. The drama had some of its most devoted supporters among these young students. Indeed, not only were "the clamorous fry of Innes of Court" well represented in the audiences at both the public and private theaters; they sometimes hired players, including Shakespeare's company, to perform on special occasions at the Inns.

Some of the student frolics also involved dramas, which the students wrote and performed.[23]

The exciting and stimulating little world of the Inns of Court was set within the larger and more varied world of Renaissance London. London must have dazzled a youth like Davies whose life had so far been lived in rural villages and in academic cloisters. The bustle of its crowded and narrow streets, its numerous shops which attracted merchants and tradesmen from all over the kingdom, and the vitality of a growing world capital contrasted sharply with the quiet of Chisgrove, Winchester, and Oxford. Contributing strongly to the vibrant interest of the city was Elizabeth's Court, the real nerve center of the kingdom, where not only decisions of great national pitch and moment were to be arrived at but where individual reputations and fortunes were also to be made (and lost) and where great preferments were always about to be conferred. To the four palaces in or near the city—Westminster, Whitehall, St. James, and the Tower—came the powerful and those aspiring to great place—including Davies—and vying for opportunities to attract the Sovereign's eye and somehow—not least through poetic talents—to win her good favor.[24]

Near at hand, too, were the amusements and enticing distractions of the growing metropolis. Only a brief boatride across the Thames from the Temple were the public playhouses, bearbaiting pits, and stews, providing ample opportunities for a mirthful and inventive group of students to take a holiday from their study of law. That Davies knew a good bit about this freer, even libertine, life of London is clear from his *Epigrams*. Published around 1595, these poems ridicule the gaucheries of London fops and wayward law students, and they record vignettes of well-known London amusements from the public stage to the brothels.

During his early years in London, Davies, like many of his fellow students, was given to "outbursts of youthful extravagance and self-indulgence." Student celebrations connected with Candlemas had actually become so disorderly that the Masters of the Bench had condemned them and admonished students from "playing dice or cards, outcries in the night, [and] breaking open chambers." Nevertheless, in 1590 several of the students, including Davies and his friends Richard Martin and William Fleetwood, "broke the ordinance by making outcries, forcibly breaking open chambers in the night and levying money as Lord of Misrule's rent, and contemptuously refused to declare the names of the others" involved with them.[25] As a consequence, the students were fined and warned that a repetition of such behavior would result in their expulsion. Apparently undismayed, on February 11 of the following year, Davies, along with Martin and Fleetwood, again "broke open chamber doors and abused many gentlemen of the House." This time Martin and Fleetwood were expelled, and Davies was ordered "out of commons during the pleasure of the Masters and Benchers."[26] They were eventually re-admitted, but only after formal petitions.

The Reverend T. C. Childs has added a very interesting item to our knowledge of Davies' life. He has found two letters written by Davies in Latin to the prominent lawyer and scholar Paul Merula.[27] The letters make clear that Davies, Martin, and Fleetwood were companions in another diversion from the law books—travel to the Continent. The first letter is endorsed by Merula "Accep. 2 May 1592"; and the second, although undated, makes clear that Davies and his companions had visited Merula in Holland. Writing to William Camden on October 20, 1592, Merula expressed his pleasure in the young men's visit.[28] In his second letter, Davies complained of his boredom with "the barbarous, wretched study of our Municipal Law, which is quite opposed to all the more humane Letters; while the merry and urbane Muses place Nectar and Ambrosia before your lordship in all profusion and abundance."[29] In the autumn of 1592, Merula was favored by the Muses in being elected to the chair of history at the University of Leiden; this led Reverend Childs to think that it was there that Davies and his party visited the scholar.

Davies had also found time to court his own urbane and merry muse of poetry. For a young man like Davies, writing poetry was an avocation, not an occupation or way of life; it was one of the graces and amenities of social life, a gentlemanly accomplishment as desirable as the ability to ride and to handle a rapier. While writing poetry no doubt afforded its own immediate pleasures to a poet, in the sixteenth century it could have an important social utility not usually associated with it today. It was an effective means of attracting attention, of displaying one's wittiness in a pungent epigram, or one's subtle sensibility in a sugared sonnet. Further, as a compliment, as part of some aristocratic entertainment, or as a significant work dedicated to someone of note, poetry was a means of promoting one's more serious career interest by winning the good will and, one hoped, the good offices of the powerful. As we shall see, much of Davies' poetry had such an extra-literary purpose, and effect.

Many of the gentlemen and courtly poets of the day felt a strong disinclination to publish their poems and showed a surprising casualness about preserving them once they had been written and enjoyed. As a consequence, much poetry of the time has no doubt been lost. While Davies did publish *Orchestra, Nosce Teipsum,* and the *Hymnes of Astraea,* much of his poetry, like that of other poets, circulated in manuscript among the poet's acquaintances. His witty verses seem to have been sought after, for many of his epigrams were copied into the manuscript commonplace books and poetical miscellanies, which it was fashionable in the day to compile.

Although precise dates of composition are difficult, if not impossible, to determine, it is probable that most of the poems for which he is remembered were written by 1597 or so. Among these are the *Epigrams, Orchestra,* and, probably, the "Gulling Sonnets," parodies of the love sonnet. Although not published until 1599, *Nosce Teipsum,* as will be shown later, was probably in large part written during this early period. Davies also composed a graceful epithalamion in honor of the wedding on January 26, 1594/1595 between Elizabeth Vere and William Stanley, members of very prominent aristocratic families. From such works Davies gained some prominence as a poet and wit. His *Epigrams* are alluded to by other poets; and, according to Wood, *Orchestra* was "much extoll'd by scholars of all sorts."[30] Something of his standing is indicated by a marginal gloss in William Covell's *Polimanteia* (1595), which lists Davies along with Thomas Campion, Nicholas Breton, Thomas Lodge, Michael Drayton, and others as a contemporary poet worthy of commendation.[31]

II *Attack and Retreat*

Despite the distractions of London and his proclivities toward riotous pranks, Davies managed to learn enough law to be called to the bar on July 4, 1595, "with the assent of all the masters of the Bench."[32] But this professional accomplishment was shortly annulled; for Davies' prospects were seriously dashed by a curiously violent act by the poet.

The details of this dramatic event, which occurred February 9, 1597, are described in the records of the Middle Temple as follows:

While the Masters of the Bench and other fellows were quietly dining publicly in the Hall, John Davyes, one of the Masters of the Bar, in cap and gown, and girt with a dagger, his servant and another with him being armed with swords, came into the Hall. The servant and the other person stayed at the bottom of the Hall, while he walked up to the fireplace and then to the lower part of the second table for Masters of the Bar, where Richard Martyn was quietly dining. Taking from under his gown a stick, which is commonly called "a Bastinado," he struck Martyn on the head with it till it broke, and then running to the bottom of the Hall he took his servant's sword out of his hand, shook it over his own head . . . and ran down to the water steps and jumped into a boat.[33]

This Richard Martin had been Davies' earlier companion in student pranks and travel, and that Davies had developed a great admiration for him is shown in the rather extravagant language of the sonnet dedicating *Orchestra* to Martin. A Devonshire man, Martin had been at Oxford at the same time as the poet and, leaving without taking a degree, was admitted to the Middle Temple in 1587.[34] A lover of the good life, Martin was reputed a wit and an amusing companion, one whose gibes, gambols, and flashes of merriment had no doubt often set the Temple tables on a roar. He won the admiration of men like John Selden, John Hoskins, Benjamin Rudyard, and Ben Jonson, who dedicated *The Poetaster* to him. He later served in Parliament and as Reader at the Middle Temple in 1615–1616 and as Recorder of London in 1618. His term as Recorder was brief, for he died shortly after taking office, as John Aubrey puts it, "of a symposiaque excesse with his fellow-witts,"[35] or as Lord Stowell more elegantly circumlocutes, "from disorders produced by his devotion to the pleasures of the table, likely enough to be incident to a man of wit and humour...."[36]

Davies' motives for so violent an attack on his companion in carousals have never been fully explained. Deliberate and public, almost ceremonial, the attack suggests a retribution for some affront to Davies' honor. The "Carte Notes" give no explanation, and Wood simply offers that, "being a high spirited young man," Davies "did, upon some little provocation or punctilio, bastinado Rich. Martin...."[37] George Chalmers reasonably speculates that the "punctilio" may well have been some inopportune wittiness at Davies' expense.[38] Most convincing has been the suggestion by P. J. Finkelpearl that Davies probably received some insult during the Christmas revels held at the Middle Temple just prior to this attack.[39] Martin had served as the leader of the festivities and, as the Prince d'Amour, had taken a very active part in the festive celebrations.

However baffling the motives, the penalties for such an audacious and intemperate act were swift and severe. According to the "Carte Notes," the poet was for a time "confined and made a prisoner," a penalty which is supported by a wry couplet in a contemporary manuscript commonplace book in the Bodleian, which reads: "Davis beinge committed to prison for a quarrell betweene him and Martin, wrote as ensueth, 'Now Davis for a birde is in / But yet it is but a Martin.' "[40] More seriously, Davies was expelled from the Middle Temple "never to return"; and he was disbarred and stripped of authority to practice law.[41] Under such a cloud Davies withdrew from London, according to the "Carte Notes" to the country but according to Wood, to Oxford where, "in the condition of a sojourner ... [he] follow'd his studies, tho' he wore a cloak."[42]

During this period of unsought leisure, Davies became interested in the revival of the Society of Antiquaries, an association of men such as Robert Cotton, John Stowe, and William Camden, who met from time to time to hear and discuss papers on historical subjects. Davies presented several papers before this group on subjects such as the history of lawful combats and the office of the High Steward of England.[43] The most interesting of his papers was read on November 3, 1600, and treated English epitaphs.[44] Although these musty pages are unlikely to interest many today, they do afford evidence of Davies' scholarly pursuits and a perspective on the leisure life of educated gentlemen of the time.

Davies also set about recovering his lost opportunities, a goal in which his muse played an important part. In 1599, he published *Nosce Teipsum*. How much of this important work Davies may have written earlier is uncertain; but, following the advice of his patron Lord Mountjoy, Davies published it with a flattering dedication to Elizabeth, "A happy angell to this happy Land," and the possessor of "the diuinest and richest minde." He followed such encomium in the same year with his *Hymnes of Astraea*, acrostic poems extolling the many virtues of the Queen.

While the immediate effect of these poetic bids for the Queen's good will is difficult to specify, the support and exertion in his behalf by men of influence are more easily demonstrated. As a genial wit, as a man of letters, or as a promising lawyer and civil servant, Davies seems to have won the regard of several men of prominence and power during his early years in London. His meeting with Paul Merula has already been noted. According to the "Carte Notes" he had been a member of an embassy sent to Scotland in 1594 in honor of the birth of Prince Henry, son of the next king of England. Three individuals who especially served him well during his period of rustication, and later in his career, were Charles Blount (1563–1606), Sir Robert Cecil (1563?–1612), and Sir Thomas Egerton (1540?–1617).[45]

Blount, Lord Mountjoy, had become one of Elizabeth's court favorites. He had studied briefly at Oxford and at the Inner Temple and had served in Parliament; but it was as a military man that he enjoyed his greatest success. In addition to other military expeditions, he distinguished himself by defeating the Irish rebel chief, the earl of Tyrone, in 1602, thereby bringing the bitter Irish war to an end. According to the "Carte Notes," Mountjoy not only urged Davies to publish *Nosce Teipsum* and to dedicate it to the Queen but also arranged for the poet to present a copy to Elizabeth.

Sir Robert Cecil, who became the first earl of Salisbury and

Viscount Cranborne during King James I's reign, was appointed Elizabeth's secretary of state in 1596, a post which he continued to hold in James's government. Although undated, the following curious letter from Davies to Cecil seems to relate to the poet's efforts towards restoration: "Righthon. S^r hauing y^r Memory charged wth so many great besonesses, there is no reason why you should remember such a Trifle as J am. howbeit the experience wch J have had of y^r honorable favour doth begett in me a strong faith & assurance that you have not forgotten me. / & therfore J should much forgett my Self, Jf J should not remember to praesent my humble Thanks & devotion vnto you who, J doubt not, like a good Angell, have er this donne me a great benefit though it be yet invisible & vnknowne vnto men."[46]

In another letter, dated June 16, 1601, Davies thanks Cecil for a "special favour" which he had shown him recently at York House. Although no tangible benefit was yet forthcoming from it, Davies says, "it reflected much grace vppon me another way. / for many that were praesent did valew me the better, when they saw so great & worthy a personage haue such respect & care of me. /" Apologizing for troubling Cecil with "so trifling a besones," he concludes by beseeching him "to cast one Sunbeame more of y^r favour vppon me in this behalf; wch if it clear not my disgrace, I will draw a clow'd over me, & so rest vntill I may overcome it either by time or by Desert."[47]

Sir Thomas Egerton, Baron Ellesmere, particularly enjoyed the high trust of Elizabeth. Lord Keeper of the Great Seal and member of the privy council, noted for his wealth, patronage of writers, and kindness to young barristers, he was a man of considerable influence.[48] In 1599, Davies had written a sonnet "On the Death of Lord Chancellor Ellesmere's second Wife," which managed both to note the passing of Lady Ellesmere and to compliment the Lord to whom "the god of Wisdome and of Loue" had imparted "Solomon's braine" and "David's tender hart."[49] Perhaps it was Davies' talents as a writer that first attracted Egerton's attention. At any rate, his interest in Davies' career lasted well into the seventeenth century, and years later the poet recalled his indebtedness to Egerton. When Davies published *Le Primer Report* (1615), he dedicated the work to his old patron and in the Preface justified his lavish tribute to him as the ideal Lord Chancellor, saying "...there is no man liuing whom it may better become than my self, to praise and honor your Lordship euery way, whose fauor hath bin (as it were) a good angell vnto me, and to whom I stand bound for so many benefits, as that which might carry a shew of adulation in another, must needs be thought but duty and gratitude in me."[50]

Wood claims that through Egerton's intercession Davies was "restored to his chamber" at the Middle Temple.[51] Evidence of the Lord Chancellor's exertion toward this end appears in a letter which he wrote June 30, 1601, to the Benchers of the Middle Temple. He notes that he had earlier "spoken pryvately vnto some of yo^u, & written to yo^u all in generall, for the restoringe of *Mr Jo: Dauis* to the benefitt of yo^{ur} societye," and marvels that he has not received an appropriate reply. He continues: "The tyme that he hath ben already sequestred from your house semeth (in mine opinion) a sufficient puñishment, and the Repentance which he hath showed, a reasonable satisfacion for his offence. Wherof I haue thought fitt once againe to putt you in minde, and ernestly to moove you to take consideracioñ. And so, expectinge now some present satisfacion from you in his behalf, I bidd you hartily farewell."[52]

Such intercessions finally brought results. Writing on July 8, 1601, John Chamberlain observed: "The Lord Cheife Justice [Sir John Popham] and Master Secretarie [Cecil] have taken great paines to compound the quarrell twixt Martin and Davies which they have effected to the satisfaction of both parts."[53] In 1601, Davies subsequently petitioned the Masters of the Middle Temple to excuse his past faults and in the fall of the same year again asked that "you wilbe pleased to forget my former indiscrecion, for which I have allreadye suffered much damage and disgrace, and to recreate and readmitt mee into the Societie...."[54] The petition was granted on condition that Davies submit on All Saints' Day a formal apology to Sir John Popham and other senior members of the Society. Accordingly, before dinner in the same great dining hall in which he had assaulted Martin, Davies professed his regrets to the assembled Templars for the "greate outrage" which he had committed and his desire that "the whole Fellowship ... [might] pardon myne offence uppon this my submission, proceeding from my hartye repentance...."[55]

Davies then turned to Martin; and, promising him his sincere love and affection in all good offices towards him in the future, he asked and received Martin's forgiveness and the restoration to his profession.

III *The Career of a Grave Lawyer*

That Davies had learned much from these trying experiences is certain. Henceforth, his energies are devoted no longer to youthful pranks or collegiate hostilities but to hard work and to a steady pursuit of professional advancement. Perhaps an outward sign of such a commitment is found in his election from Corfe Castle in 1601 to the last Parliament of Elizabeth's reign. The principal debate in this Parliament was the question of monopolies whereby the Queen had permitted favored individuals to exact a levy on certain items of trade or manufacture. Surprising in view of his later defense of royal prerogatives, Davies supported Parliament's privileges in controlling such practices. When the Queen, reluctantly, acceded to Parliament's views in this matter, Davies was appointed to a special committee of the House commissioned to thank her for withdrawing certain of the more unpopular patents.

During the next few years, Davies' poetry remained popular, for new editions of *Nosce Teipsum* appeared in 1602 and 1608. And a number of his poems were included by Francis Davison in his famous anthology *A Poetical Rhapsody*; among these were *Ten Sonets to Philomel,* "A Hymne in Praise of Musicke," and *Yet Other Twelve Wonders of the World.* But the volume of his poetry, as well as its interest, markedly declined as Davies' professional career gained momentum. Aside from his "metaphrase" of the Psalms written towards the end of his life, his poetry became chiefly "occasional"—poems written for some public event or works devised as entertainments for aristocratic gatherings. For example, Davies wrote *A Lotterie* and *A Contention betwixt a Wife, a Widdow, and a Maide* to entertain Elizabeth on visits to the houses of Egerton in 1601 and Cecil in 1602, and he composed poetic welcomes to England for James and his Queen. Although the next twenty-five years are of little direct interest to the student of Davies' poetry, they

are worth a brief consideration since his activities and interests
help to place his earlier poetry in perspective in terms of the
man's many talents.

A turning point in Davies' career came with the reign of James
I. Shortly after the Queen's death in March, 1603, Davies was
among a group led by Lord Hunsdon who hurried to Scotland
to inform James VI of Scotland, soon to be James I of England,
concerning the news and to pledge their allegiance to the new
monarch. The overt play for attention annoyed some observers in
London; for example John Chamberlain, writing in March, 1603,
expressed his disapproval of such self-serving activities: "There
is much posting that way and many run thether of theyre owne
errand, as yf yt were nothing els but first come first served, or
that preferment were a goale to be got by footmanship. . . ."[56]

But, in the scramble for royal attention, while preferments
and choice appointments were yet to be made, the advantage of
such early contacts with the king was obvious. Francis Bacon,
seeking vicarious participation in Davies' pilgrimage, wrote
the poet, desiring him "to perform to [Bacon] all the good offices,
if there be any nibbling at my name, which the vivacity of your
wit can suggest to be performed to one in whose affections
you have so great sympathy, and in whose fortune you have so
great interest."[57] Davies' aspiring heart must have been warmed
when James recognized him in Lord Hunsdon's group as the
author of *Nosce Teipsum* and "graciously embraced him."[58] In
April, 1603, still annoyed at "the Concourse of ydle and uneces-
sarie posters into Scotland, the number whereof grew to be a
great burthen to the countrie," Chamberlain noted that "John
Davies is sworne his [the King's] man."[59] To the royal compliment
to Davies' poetry was added a royal appointment; for on November 25, 1603, the King appointed Davies his Solicitor in Ireland.[60]
Davies proceeded to Ireland in the company of his patron Lord
Mountjoy, the Lord-Deputy of Ireland, to embark upon a new
and important phase in his career.

Although historians differ—usually depending on whether they
are English or Irish—in praising or damning Davies' work in
Ireland, it is generally conceded that he played a very important
role in shaping and executing Anglo-Irish policies during the
next fifteen years. While a comprehensive treatment of his career

would take us too far away from the principal concern of the present study, a brief account suggests something of the man's abilities. On arriving in Ireland, Davies plunged into his work with enormous energy and unreserved commitment.[61] And the Ireland to which he came required such qualities as his if the English were ever to consolidate their hold on this primitive, beautiful land. In the closing months of Elizabeth's reign, after years of costly and depleting war, the English forces had finally won a military victory and exacted a public surrender from the great Irish chieftain Hugh O'Neill. But the difficult task of establishing and preserving an order compatible with English ideas and requirements still had to be begun.

In the early years of his reign, James sought to integrate Ireland as a real part of his kingdom. He endeavored to do so by imposing English political ideals upon the Irish, by enforcing the common law, by modifying the ancient system of land tenure, by restraining the Catholic faithful, and by strengthening the effectiveness of the established church. Towards these ends Davies devoted himself with great drive and, in his superiors' views, with great effect.

First as Solicitor and then in 1606 as Attorney-General, Davies spent much of his time traveling throughout Ireland. As Commissioner of the Assize, much of his travel was designed to impose an English justice on Irish felons, a feat which was accomplished sometimes in a swift and harsh manner. In addition to "delivering the gaols" of those awaiting trial, Davies and his companions surveyed and mapped counties, adjudicated a varied assortment of disputes, examined titles to church properties and crown lands, sought to establish local free schools, and attempted to expedite the transfer of feudal allegiances from local chieftains to the English king.

For the appreciative enlightenment of his superiors, as well as later students of Anglo-Irish history, Davies recorded his impressions and experiences during these tiring and potentially dangerous journeys in a voluminous official and personal correspondence and in somewhat more formal papers of observation and description.[62] Sensitive and lucid, his accounts are not only highly informative but sometimes keenly vivid. He was moved by the wild beauty of the land, intrigued by its unusual customs and practices, and saddened by the miseries of famine, outlawry, and pestilence which the Irish peasants, caught between two historical and political ages, suffered. His on-the-scene reporting was highly valuable to officials in England who depended upon such information to formulate their plans. Writing in 1606, Salisbury acknowledged Davies' useful information-gathering activities:

I have received from you so good a relation of the proceedings in both your circuits, as I must confess doth yield me very great contentment; first because I see it is sperable by a Christian policy without rigour or exorbitant charge to work some of those happy effects in the land of Ire, which are found in the land of promise; next because you have so perfectly described or rather anatomised, all those parts wherein you have travelled, and the disposition of the people, as will give me more light to direct my counsels upon many occasions than any other kind of advertisement. . . .[63]

In the records of the times, Davies figures prominently in two especially important undertakings: the Ulster Plantation settlement and the calling into session of the Irish Parliament in 1613.

The Irish peace was always precarious in these years because of the lingering loyalty of the Irish to their chieftains and the chieftains' ambitions to regain control and, perhaps through alliances with Continental Catholic powers, to expel the English. Two such chieftains were the earls of Tyrone and Tyrconnell, who for reasons never completely explained—some think because of their involvement in an abortive attempt to seize Dublin Castle and to instigate a general rebellion—fled to the Continent in 1607, where it was rumored they were attempting to raise support. Designated by historians as "the flight of the Earls," this flight was regarded by the English as treason, for which the earls were indicted in absentia.

An important consequence of their actions was the crown's confiscation of their huge land holdings in Ulster, which consisted of the counties of Armagh, Cavan, Coleraine, Donegal, Fermanagh, and Tyrone. The crown carefully worked out a scheme for the redistribution of these lands by making grants to the English faithful, by selling huge tracts to English speculators, and by assigning tracts to those Irish whose docility and quiet acquiescence could be depended upon. The Ulster settlement, in whose formulation and execution (both in Ireland and in the councils in London), Davies played a leading part, sought to colonize Ulster with Protestant English settlers whose allegiance would strengthen the king's control over this important area of Ireland. While the English seemed pleased with the outcome and prospects of this plantation, Irish sympathizers have never forgotten the injustices involved, including Davies' efforts, nor have sober historians ignored the enmity and bitternesses against England which this scheme aroused, bitternesses which flare up to this very day in Northern Ireland.

As a means of confirming and gaining legal sanction for the Ulster settlement and of establishing law and legislative procedure, James I and his advisors called the Irish Parliament into session. Such an action involved many difficulties, for no Parliament had met since 1586; and few, if any, of the men likely to be its members in 1613 had had any parliamentary experience. In addition, the records relating to precedents and procedures were scanty. But with his characteristic vigor, Davies set about investigating the history of the Irish parliaments, the conditions under which they had been called into session, and the numbers who had composed them. This information aided him in planning for the Parliament and was incorporated into the address which he made on its opening as Speaker and as representative for Fermanagh.

A more difficult question was the makeup of the representatives, especially in the House of Commons. In order for the Parliament to serve the king's purposes, a Protestant majority likely to support royal policies had to be assured. To promote such a majority, the king created new constituencies whose representatives could safely be counted in his camp. The recusants' opposition to this stratagem was strong and at the very beginning of the sessions in May 18, 1613, provoked a stormy episode concerning the election of the Speaker. Davies had been returned as the first representative of Fermanagh and was nominated as Speaker; Sir John Everard, a former Irish judge who had resigned because he declined to subscribe to the Oath of Supremacy, was the candidate for the Roman Catholics.

In the election, Davies won a clear majority; but the Catholics contested the results, objecting to the king's creation of new boroughs and to the election of members not residents of the places which had returned them. They installed Everard in the Speaker's chair and refused its occupancy to Davies. Only after some undignified scuffling was Everard dislodged and Davies seated in the Speaker's chair.

Despite the uproar and hostility to him, Davies assumed the office of Speaker and delivered a lengthy address, expressing the hope that the present Parliament would confirm and establish the blessings of peace and obedience "together with plenty, civility, and other felicities ... unto us, and to make them perpetual to our posterities."[64]

In the months which followed, the recusants seemed to have been conciliated and their cooperation with the Parliament gained. In a second speech, on October 11, 1614, Davies congratulated the House for its cooperation and developed one of his favorite analogies for social order and peace:

[James I] finding the strings of his harp of Ireland in discord and out of tune, hath not by hard wresting broken them, but by gentle and easy winding brought them to a concord; and though in the tuning of this instrument there hath been a little jarring and harshness at the first, yet now the strings are set right by so happy and skilful a hand, we hope the music that shall follow shall be the sweeter. For I, for my part, did never doubt but that of that stormy beginning there would come a calm end, and after our blustering forenoon we should have a fair afternoon.[65]

Davies' correspondence with Salisbury in this period indicates that he was very much pleased with the results of Davies' work in the Irish Parliament. Davies was not without his reward for his earnest service to the Crown. From Solicitor-General in 1603 he had been promoted to Attorney-General in 1606 and named Serjeant-at-Law in Ireland in the same year. Knighted, he became *Sir* John Davies in 1603 and was named Serjeant-at-Law in England in 1612. Legal fees from these offices added to his wealth, as did thousands of acres of land grants in Ireland.[66]

While in Ireland, Davies also acquired a wife. The precise date of his marriage is uncertain; but on March 3, 1609, John

Chamberlain reported that Davies is "lincked with a daughter of the Lord Audleyes."[67] The lady was Eleanor Touchet, youngest daughter of George, Lord Audeley, Earl of Castlehaven; Davies probably first met his bride at her father's house while riding circuit as judge of assize. Said by her biographer George Ballard to have had "a learned education,"[68] Lady Eleanor seems to have lived happily with her scholarly husband, who was some twenty years her senior. Although mention is usually made of only two children, the "Carte Notes" assert that two sons and a daughter were born of this union: John, mentally defective, and Richard, both of whom "dyed young," and Lucy, born on January 20, 1612, who eventually married Ferdinando, Lord Hastings, who became the sixth Earl of Huntingdon.[69]

During these eventful years Davies somehow found time to complete a substantial work in political history entitled *A Discoverie of the Trve Cavses why Ireland was neuer entirely Subdued, nor brought vnder Obedience of the Crowne of England*. Published in 1612 and dedicated to James I, the work is a highly readable account of past failures and present successes of Anglo-Irish policy.[70] Beginning with the reign of Henry II, Davies analyzes the errors committed by a succession of English governments, the various attempts to remedy them, and, finally, the success of James I's government in righting past wrongs and in supplying present needs.

Another of Davies' scholarly works was published in 1615 in Dublin. Written in law French, *Le Primer Report des Cases et Matters in Ley . . . en Ireland* is a collection of "selected Cases, which since the beginning of his Maiesties Raigne haue been argued, resolued, & adiudged in this Realme of Ireland." They constituted, according to Davies, "the first Report of Cases arising in Ireland & ruled in the Courts of Iustice there, that euer was made & published to the world, since the lawes of England were first established in this kingdome."

The chief interest of *Le Primer Report* for most modern readers is its preface, addressed to Davies' loyal supporter, Lord Ellesmere.[71] In it, Davies defends his profession against the "vulgar *imputations* cast vppon the *lawe* & *lawiers*"; discusses the concept of Common Law; and, like many of his thoughtful contemporaries, writes eloquently upon the benefits of social order and the horrors of social disorder and the place of law and justice in the preservation of society. In the final pages, Davies depicts those qualities which an ideal Lord Chancellor, as the chief representative of justice and law, should possess. Not surprisingly, he concludes that Ellesmere matches the ideal at all points. As an expression of his admiration and gratitude, he dedicates his book, "the first-fruits of [his] labour in this kinde of learning," to his "good angell."[72]

During his years in Ireland, Davies had visited England on several occasions. More than once he had expressed to Salisbury the hope that his appointment might be terminated; and he was at length officially recalled in 1619. In England, he continued his professional life as a lawyer, served in 1620–21 as justice of assize, and sat in Parliament in 1621 for Newcastle-under-Lyne. In 1622, he published in a single volume *Orchestra, Hymnes of Astraea,* and *Nosce Teipsum.* His continuing scholarly interests are reflected in such works as his *Abridgement* of Sir Edward Coke's *Reports* and a treatise entitled *The Question concerning Impositions, Tonnage, Poundage, Prizage, Customs,* both published posthumously. Whether the attribution is correct or not, Grosart printed as Davies' *A New Post: With Soueraigne salue to cure the Worlds madnes.*[73] According to the title page, the author is "Sir *I. D.* Knight." Published in 1620, the work consists of seven essays treating such subjects as number, place, and time; and one poem, "Reason's Moane," which lauds James I, and in its denigration of human reason recalls Elegy I of *Nosce Teipsum.* A. H. Bullen has, however, challenged the attribution of *A New Post* to Davies.[74]

IV *Return to England*

The closing months of Davies' life were troubled by the bizarre conduct of his wife.[75] Around 1625, Lady Eleanor underwent a religious experience from which she never quite recovered. Her "voices," her sometimes unintelligible utterances and writings, and her eccentric behavior would stamp her today as dangerously neurotic and as intermittently insane. But Lady Eleanor, convinced that she had been singled out as God's Prophetess and directed to enlighten the darkness of her day, embarked upon a fervent career which was to bring her fame and grief. In view of Davies' conservative attitudes toward religion and the authority of the established church, his impatience with such evangelical enthusiasms would be predictable. In one of her pamphlets, *The Lady Eleanor her Appeal* (1646), she recalls that her husband once burned a manuscript of her prophecies. She retaliated by prophesying that within three years Davies might expect his "mortal blow." With characteristic confidence, she donned her mourning garments. Three days before Davies' sudden death and, as she maintains, in the presence of his friends and servants, she "gave him pass to take his long sleep. . . ." The startling accuracy of her predictions must later have qualified the wittiness of her husband's reply: "I pray weep not while I am alive, and I will give you leave to laugh when I am dead."[76]

Soon after the death of James I in 1625, Davies was diligently at work ingratiating himself with the new king: "As soone as I heard of the death of *K: James* I came vp from Englefeild to kisse *K: Charles'* his hands and to renew my Patent of Kinges Serjeant both wch I haue done this day."[77] Almost immediately, Charles came into conflict with Parliament by attempting to force loans to alleviate his financial problems. When the Lord Chief Justice Sir Randolph Crew refused to approve the legality of the king's demands, he was discharged from his post. In reward perhaps for Davies' years of service, but more likely because he had written in support of the king's right to force such loans, Davies was nominated for the prestigious position of Lord Chief Justice. Shortly before he expected to take office, however, "he died suddenly in his house in the Strand near to London, in the 57th year of his age the 7th of December, in sixteen hundred twenty and six, found dead in his bed, by an apoplexy, as 'twas said."[78]

After the body had lain in state for some time, "it was convey'd to the church of St. Martin in the Fields near to Whitehall, where it was solemnly inter'd in the South-isle."[79] According to the "Carte Notes," Davies' former fellow law student, John Donne, then the distinguished Dean of St. Paul's Cathedral, delivered the funeral sermon.

CHAPTER 2

"Our English Martial"

A new spirit began to pervade much of English literature during the 1590's. The escapist world of pastoral verse and romance, conjuring up images of a timeless and effortless life of love and friendship, and the sonneteers' extravagant idealizations of imaginary mistresses, extolling their physical and spiritual beauties, sometimes in wearying clichés, gave way to works inspired by the caustic muse of satire and to more colloquial, even vulgar, styles. Established literary forms like the lyric and sonnet were adapted to new and surprising uses and subjected by writers like John Donne and Davies to burlesque and parodic treatments. Verse satirists, such as Joseph Hall and John Marston, sometimes in coarse and deliberately shocking language, snarled at the rapacities and sinister follies of their fellows. And the powerful example of Ben Jonson's "humorous" satirical comedies —designed to ridicule and, hopefully, thereby to amend the imprudent conduct of man—began to rival Shakespeare's romantic comedies.[1] As Barnabe Rich observed, "many excellent wittes [were] endeavoring by their pennes to set upp lightes, & to give the world new eyes to see into deformitie."[2]

This development in cultural history is well known, and several theories have been proposed to account for it. Some see the interest in satirical writing primarily as a literary phenomenon springing from a Humanist interest in imitating Classical satirists like Juvenal and Martial. Others stress sociological factors such as the interest of a growing middle-class reading audience in more realistic works treating subjects more related to its concerns and in a more familiar style of language. Still others have related the new critical spirit to the psychology of the period, to its concern about Elizabeth's successor, and to a state of *fin de siècle* depression and melancholy induced by the passing of an

38

old order and its great figures and apprehension about what and who were to take their places.[3]

Perhaps all of these concerns played some part in the intellectual and attitudinal climate of this period. On a simpler level, however, the early attraction to satirical writing for young wits like Harington, Donne, and Davies may have been more a reaction to what had immediately gone before than to any acute distress over social ills or profound disillusionment. Popular literary modes and forms in time beget reactions, marked styles invite parody, and widely revered works call for travesties. Satire and sardonic comment probably appeared to the young wits of the Inns of Court as modish ways of gaining attention and of demonstrating their keen perceptions of the foibles of others and their superiority to such out-of-date sentiments as romantic love and its lyric celebrations in undiscriminating, sugared styles. Whatever the causes of such attitudes, Davies' *Epigrams* are a manifestation of this vigorous satirical spirit of the 1590's—perhaps not only a manifestation but even one of its contributing causes.

I *The* Epigrams

Writing epigrams was probably among Davies' earliest literary activities after his arrival in London. Although the chronology of his early poems cannot be absolutely fixed, the epigrams were probably the first of his work to be published; but establishing the date of their first publication poses some vexing bibliographical problems. Six different early editions have been identified.[4] With minor variations the title pages read: *"Epigrammes and Elegies. By I. D. and C. M. At Middleborough."* The *"Elegies"* are Christopher Marlowe's translation of Ovid's *Amores,* and they appear with the *Epigrams* in each of these editions. The title page gives no indication of date, and scholarly guesses have ranged from 1590 to 1600. That the *Epigrams* had been printed by 1599 is certain, for in June of that year the Bishop of London and the Archbishop of Canterbury ordered that "Davyes Epigrams, with Marlowe's Elegyes" be burned, along with other objectionable works.[5] More precise dating must rest on internal evidence of the *Epigrams* themselves. In recent

years, J. M. Nosworthy has noted topical allusions in two of
the *Epigrams* which would preclude their having been printed
prior to 1594.[6] Epigram 4 mentions Sir Francis Vere's conquest
of Groningen, an event which occurred in 1594; and Epigram
6 refers to the "Water Works" in London, constructed in 1594.
Nosworthy's suggestion of 1595 seems therefore a likely date of
publication for the first edition.[7]

One other matter might be mentioned concerning the publication of the *Epigrams*. Middleborough, or Middleburg, as a
place of publication has sometimes been regarded as a printer's
ruse "in the issuance of a book which quite certainly could not
have been licensed" for publication.[8] There may also be some
light mockery involved because Middleburg was a town from
which Puritan pamphlets were frequently issued,[9] hardly the
sort of interest catered to in the *Amores* or in Davies' *Epigrams*.
But it may be that, following his visits to Holland in 1592,
Davies, or one of his friends, actually arranged for foreign
publication of the work. It has even been suggested, although
not very convincingly, that Ben Jonson, who had fought in the
Low Countries, played some role in publishing the volume in
Holland.[10]

The epigram had been very popular in Europe during the
fourteenth and fifteenth centuries as a vehicle for a brief compliment, commemorative inscription, gnomic observation, satiric
quip, and lampoon. The famous historian Jacob Burckhardt,
writing of the Italian Renaissance, observed: "The Latin epigram
finally became ... an affair of serious importance, since a few
clever lines, engraved on a monument or quoted with laughter in
society, could lay the foundation of a scholar's celebrity."[11]
During the early sixteenth century, the epigram was cultivated
as an academic exercise in English schools; and, as noted earlier,
Martial was among the Classical authors studied at Winchester
College, where the writing of epigrams seems to have been
an important part of the school's curriculum. In addition to
Davies, several well-known Elizabethan epigrammatists were
trained at Winchester, including Thomas Bastard, John Hoskins,
John Owen, and John Heath.[12] While Sir Thomas More earned
scholarly praise for his learnedly witty Latin epigrams and
while others, such as John Heywood, wrote epigrams in English

during the middle years of the century, not until the last two decades did the epigram come into vogue.

Timothe Kendall, a law student at Staples Inn, published an important anthology of epigrams in 1577. Entitled *The Flowers of Epigrammes*, the large volume contained translations of Classical writers, including Martial, as well as work from more recent writers like More and George Buchanan. Kendall's book helped remind his readers of the potentials of this genre and thereby, perhaps, stimulated a renewed interest in writing epigrams. Throughout the 1580's and into the 1590's, Sir John Harington, courtier and translator of Ariosto, wrote a large number of epigrams. Although they were not published until after his death in 1612, they circulated among his acquaintances in manuscript and were copied into commonplace books for others to read. They earned for their young author a considerable reputation as a wit, and the recognition they brought him probably encouraged others to seek similar attention through a display of their epigrammatic cleverness. Davies was Harington's most notable and immediate successor. Like Harington's, Davies' epigrams circulated in manuscript[13] and drew frequent notice from other writers like Harington, Guilpin, Thomas Bastard, Ben Johnson, J. Ashton, Thomas Campion, and Henry Fitzgeoffrey. Their publication gave them even wider currency, which probably helped to establish the great vogue for the epigram during the next decades. From around 1595 until 1630 or so, more than fifty volumes of epigrams came from the London presses.[14]

The Classical precedents for the Renaissance writers of epigrams were the *Greek Anthology* and Martial's epigrams, which had treated a wide range of subject matter and employed a number of tones. In Ben Jonson's *Epigrammes* (1616), which Jonson described as "the ripest of his studies," a broad spectrum of subject and tone is represented, from two-line quips and anecdotes to satiric portraits of usurers, bawds, and English fops, from tributes to King James, the Earl of Salisbury, and other notables, to tenderly moving memorials on the deaths of Jonson's first son and a daughter, and the gifted boy-actor Salomon Pavy.[15] Such breadth was not, however, typical of most English epigrammatists; for the mocking, satiric, sometimes cyni-

cal Martial seems to have influenced Davies and most of his
fellow epigrammatists like Harington, Donne, Guilpin, John
Weaver, Samuel Rowlands, and Henry Parrot, in whose work
the close alliance of the epigram with satiric purpose is apparent. By the time Jonson published his *Epigrammes,* the term
epigram had come principally to mean, as Jonson somewhat
disapprovingly observed, a work which was "bold, licentious,
full of gall, / Wormewood, and sulphure, sharpe and tooth'd
withall."[16] Davies' practice would support Robert Hayman's
assertion:

Satyrs and Epigrams

Satyrs are Epigrams; but larger drouen
Epigrams Satrys are, but closer wouen:
An Epigram must be Satyricall,
A Satyr must be Epigrammicall.[17]

That Martial was Davies' Classical precedent (in subject matter if not in stylistic qualities) for taxing vices deserving of public blame was noted by several of his contemporaries. Everard
Guilpin, who recognized the literary paternity of the famous
Latin poet in Davies' work, named him "Our English Martial."[18]
The authors of the *Parnassus Plays* (1598–1601) saw the relationships, too, when they wrote:

Acute *John Davies,* I affect thy rimes,
That jerck in hidden charmes these looser times:
Thy playner verse thy unaffected vaine,
Is graced with a fayer and sooping trayne.
Martiall & hee may sit upon one bench,
Either wrote well & either lov'd his wench.[19]

Sir John Harington defended his and Davies' debt to Martial
against charges of plagiarism:

To *Mr*:   Iohn Dauys.

My deer *Davys,* some against vs partiall
Have found we steall some good conceits from Martiall;
So though they graunt our verse hath some Acumen,
Yet make they fooles suspect we skant ar trew men.

But *Surrey* did the same, and worthy *Wyatt*,
And they had praise and reputation by it.
And *Heywood*, whome your putting down hath raised,
Did vse the same and with the same is praised.
Wherfore yf they had witt that soe did trace vs,
They must again for their own creddits grace vs,
 Or else to our more honour and their greevs
 Match vs at least with honorable theevs.[20]

There are significant differences between Martial and Davies as epigrammatists. The Roman poet's range of subjects and tonal effects is considerably larger than that found in Davies' work, and his satirical wit is more punishing. But, in the mocking treatment of Roman figures in Martial's epigrams, Davies probably found a suggestion for a similar series of amusing portraits of London types. Clear echoes of Martial in some of Davies' *Epigrams* are evidence of more specific indebtedness. For examples, Davies' Cineas' insistence (Ep. 23) that any person he greets must first doff his hat to him recalls Martial's Naevolus' refusal to say "good day" until he is first greeted (III, xcv); and Davies' Gella's total dependency upon cosmetics and fancy costumes for her semblance of beauty (Ep. 26) finds a parallel with Martial's Galla's lack of natural endowments (IX, xxxvii). Davies' recommendation (Ep. 11) that Gella not smile at his rhymes lest she reveal her ugly teeth has precedent in Martial's similar suggestion to Maximina (II, xli); and Davies' description of Fuscus' daily round of pleasures (Ep. 28) suggests a comparable routine of Martial's Euphemus (IV, viii). Davies seems, therefore, to have first found a suggestion for a character or a situation in Martial which he then developed with details of sixteenth-century English life. His adaptation of one of Martial's epigrams can be seen in Epigram 32, in which Brunus, like Martial's Zoilus, becomes ill in order to display his fancy bed clothing to his visitors.

Martial (II,xvi)

Zoilus is ill: it is his bed-trappings
cause this fever. Suppose him well; what
will be the use of scarlet coverlets? What

of a mattress from Nile, or of one dipped in
strong-smelling purple of Sidon? What but illness
displays such foolish wealth? What do
you want with doctors? Dismiss all your
physicians. Do you wish to become well?
Take my bed-trappings.

          ✿   ✿   ✿

In Brunum.   32

Brunus, which deems himselfe a faire sweet youth
Is thirty nine yeares of age at least;
Yet was he neuer, to confesse the truth,
But a dry starveling when he was at best:
This gull was sicke to shew his night-cap fine,
And his wrought pillow over-spread with lawne;
    But hath been well since his grief's cause hath line
    At Trollup's by Saint Clement's Church, in pawne.[21]

Many of Davies' fellow wits in London knew Martial as well
as he did, and they would probably not have been disturbed by
the accusations of literary theft which Harington speaks of in
his epigram above. Recognizing an echo of Martial would have
afforded its own pleasures, and Davies' adroit adaptation of this
Classical author would, no doubt, have earned their admiration. We see in this instance a good example of the kind of effect
the so-called "revival of interest in classical culture" could have:
it provided a tradition of thought and literary form for adaptation and development by an individual talent.

Quite likely, Davies wrote many more epigrams than those
published in 1595. The principal manuscript collections contain
several not included in the printed editions; and it is probable
that a number of epigrams, the casual creations of a moment
written with little further view to permanence than a momentary
and approving smile among friends, were lost as they passed
from one reader to another.[22] But the published collection gives
a fair example of Davies' work in this genre. The *Epigrams* open
with an address to the poet's "merry Muse" and with an overview
of the subjects he will treat:

Ad Musam. 1.

Fly, merry Muse unto that merry towne,
Where thou maist playes, revels, and triumphs see;
The house of Fame, and theater of renowne,
Where all good wits and spirits loue to be.
Fall in betweene their hands that loue and praise thee,
And be to them a laughter and a jest:
But as for them which scorning shall reproue thee,
Disdaine their wits, and thinke thine [own] the best:
But if thou finde any so grose and dull,
That thinke I do to priuate taxing leane,
Bid him go hang, for he is but a gull,
And knows not what an Epigramme does meane;
Which taxeth, under a peculiar name,
A generall vice, which merits publick blame.[23]

The forty-seven epigrams which follow vary in length from four to twenty-four lines in iambic-pentameter verse with varying rhyme patterns. Over three-fourths of them end with rhyming couplets, giving an effective snap to the turn of thought toward which the epigram proceeds. A good example of this effect is the following:

In Quintum. 12.

Quintus his wit infused into his braine,
Mislikes the place, and fled into his feet;
And there it wandered up and downe the street,
Dabled in the dirt, and soakèd in the raine;
    Doubtlesse his wit intends not to aspire,
    Which leaues his head, to travell in the mire.

Another matter of form is particularly interesting, for eight of the epigrams are sonnets—an adaptation of the sonnet apparently unique with Davies.[24]

The collection is unified by its rather narrow focus on London subjects and by the poet's prevailing attitude toward them. The principal targets of these "laughing rimes" are the pretenses and follies of London dandies and of Inns of Court wastrels, those whom Davies groups under the rubric of "gulls":

Of a Gull. 2.

Oft in my laughing rimes, I name a Gull:
But this new terme will many questions breed;
Therefore at first I will expresse at full,
Who is a true and perfect Gull indeed:
A Gull is he who feares a veluet gowne,
And, when a wench is braue, dares not speak to her;
A Gull is he which trauerseth the towne,
And is for marriage known a common woer;
A Gull is he which while he proudly weares,
A siluer-hilted rapier by his side;
Indures the lyes and knocks about the eares,
Whilst in his sheath his sleeping sword doth bide:
A Gull is he which weares good handsome cloaths,
And stands, in Presence, stroaking up his haire,
And fills up his unperfect speech with oaths,
But speaks not one wise word throughout the yeare:
But to define a Gull in termes precise,—
A Gull is he which seemes, and is not wise.[25]

Except for an occasional spirited vehemence, as in Epigram
19, *"In Cineam,"* in which Davies catalogues Cineas' many dog-
like characteristics, the poet's prevailing tone is confidently tol-
erant, amused, perhaps smug, as he contemplates the gaucheries
of his inferiors. With a sophisticated equanimity skillfully rein-
forced by an informal, genuinely colloquial style, Davies records
Afer's gossipy activities as he hastens to the Burse "Twice euery
day, the newest newes to hear"—and immediately to tell (Ep. 40);
Francus' masochistic "solace with his whore" (Ep. 33); or the
routinized daily slough of Fuscus, rising each day at ten, proceeding to an ordinary "where he doth eate till one," sees "a
play till sixe," dines at seven, and retires, only to repeat a
similar cycle the following day (Ep. 39). In contrast to Martial's
acerbic wit, Juvenal's or Hall's harsh outrage, or the almost
hysterical wrath of Marston, Davies' attitude is an easy-going,
lightly cynical bemusement at the ways of the London "gulls"
and the imperfect submergence of the clod, hypocrite, and self-
indulgent in the social roles they attempt to play.

Some of the Epigrams (nos. 11, 14, and 21, for example) are
little more than versified anecdotes and jests, but many of them

are pointed portraits of Elizabethan social types, frequently posed against interestingly detailed backgrounds of Elizabethan life. Epigram 3 affords a good example of such a portrait as the insufferably superior Rufus disdains to be a part of the crowd at the theater but finds no difficulty in sharing the common entertainments provided by the brothels:

In Ruffum. 3.

Rufus the Courtier at the Theater,
Leaving the best and most conspicuous place,
Doth either to the stage himselfe transferre,
Or through a grate doth shew his double face:
For that the clamorous fry of Innes of Court,
Fills up the priuate roomes of greater price:
And such a place where all may haue resort,
He in his singularity doth dispise.
Yet doth not his particular humour shun
The common stews and brothells of the towne,
Though all the world in troops doe hither run,
Cleane and uncleane, the gentle and the clowne:
   Then why should Rufus in his pride abhorre,
   A common seate, that loues a common whore.

Epigram 47 is a good example of what Theodore Spencer has called "that medicinable ray of realism" which displays the hollowness of pretense or sham attitude.[26] The brooding melancholy *poseur,* we discover, is not absorbed in darkened thoughts about issues of genuine concern and moment in Davies' time; he worries about the impression his melancholy garb makes on others and about the trivia of his contemplated activities:

Meditations of a Gull. 47.

See, yonder melancholy gentleman,
Which, hood-wink'd with his hat, alone doth sit!
Thinke what he thinks, and tell me if you can,
What great affaires troubles his little wit.
He thinks not of the warre 'twixt France and Spaine,
Whether it be for Europe's good or ill,
Nor whether the Empire can itselfe maintaine
Against the Turkish power encroaching still;

Nor what great towne in all the Netherlands,
The States determine to beseige this Spring;
Nor how the Scottish policy now stands,
Nor what becomes of the Irish mutining.
But he doth seriously bethinke him whether
Of the gull'd people he be more esteem'd
For his long cloake or for his great black feather,
By which each gull is now a gallant deem'd;
Or of a journey he deliberates,
To Paris-garden, Cock-pit or the Play;
Or how to steale a dog he meditates,
Or what he shall unto his mistriss say:
      Yet with these thoughts he thinks himself most fit
      To be of counsell with a king for wit.

Although these satiric portraits hardly transcend their own age and lack the enduring relevance of Chaucer's sketches in the *General Prologue* or Alexander Pope's in the *Dunciad,* the relevance of whose subjects is almost daily renewed in contemporary counterparts, the *Epigrams* often provide interesting vignettes of Elizabethan life. We learn something of the theater and other less wholesome London amusements in epigrams 3, 7, 17, 28, 39, and 47. Particularly memorable is the following scene of London life, as Davies offers analogies to the way Philo is gaining the public's confidence in his questionable "practise of Physicke":

As doth the Ballad-singer's auditory,
Which hath at Temple-barre his standing chose,
And to the vulgar sings an Ale-house story:
First stands a Porter; then an Oyster-wife
Doth stint her cry, and stay her steps to heare him;
Then comes a Cut-purse ready with a knife,
And then a Countrey clyent passeth neare him;
There stands the Constable, there stands the whore.
And, listening to the song, heed not each other;
There by the Serjeant stands the debitor,
And doth no more mistrust him then his brother:
Thus Orpheus to such hearers giueth musick,
And Philo to such patients giueth physick.   (Ep. 38)

Despite Davies' insistence that he does not "to priuate taxing lean"—an "out" claimed by other satirists of the day—real figures more than likely unconsciously sat for many of these satiric portraits. In a series of his epigrams preserved in Bodleian MS. Rawlinson Poetry 212, two appear which were not included in the early printed editions; and these name individuals, presumably Nicholas Breton and Anthony Munday:

In Bretton.

Breton, though thou wert vexed with *the* Rheume
     Or, with *the* Neopolitan disease
     Or with *the* cough *that* doth the lungs consume
     Or with *the* tickling murre, or all of these
Yet Bretton knowe *that* it were farre vnfitt
     for thee, at every woord thou speakest to spitte.

❂   ❂   ❂

In Mundayum.

Munday I sweare shallbee a hollidaye
     If he forsweare himselfe but once a daye.[27]

Explicit mention of real individuals occurs in two of the *Epigrams*. In No. 29, Davies notes with some self-commendation that his "light Muse" has put down John Heywood's *Epigrams* in the public esteem. And, in Epigram 22, the allusion to "old George Gascoine's rimes" marks Ciprius' out-of-date literary taste. Decius of Epigram 25, who added his beloved to the other "nine woorthies," was identified as Michael Drayton by Ben Jonson;[28] and Samuel Daniel seems a likely candidate for the Dacus of Epigram 30, who "Amongst the poets . . . numbred is, / Yet could he neuer make an English rime."[29] Jonson, who had had military experience in Flanders, has been suggested as the Gallus of Epigram 24, and Sir Water Raleigh as Paulus in Epigram 41.[30] It is probable that Davies' intimates were able to match the figures of Publius, "a student at the Common-law" (Epigram 43), with a fellow-student at one of the Inns and knew the identity of "lousie Ponticus" (Epigram 48), who envied Davies' fame as a poet. Such knowledge would have given the collection a special piquancy for those in the know—or those who thought they were.

The *Epigrams* won Davies a reputation as a sharp and merry wit. They are alluded to more often by his contemporaries than any other of his works, and the six early editions, plus the number of manuscript collections, attest to their popularity. It is interesting, however, that, in later and more sober years, Davies omitted them in the collection of his poetry which appeared in 1622. We can understand that a grave and famous lawyer might not wish to revive such witty poems of his youth, but the *Epigrams* are still entertaining in their own right and reflect a significant light on the concerns of the time in which they were written. And we can already discern in this work Davies' developing talent for the lucid, concise writing and for the artful melding of idea with poetic form which are displayed more impressively in *Orchestra* and *Nosce Teipsum*.

II   *The* Gulling Sonnets

In addition to the social satire of the *Epigrams*, Davies wrote some clever literary parodies. Incidental comment on literary figures appeared, as we have just seen, in the *Epigrams*. In some printed editions of these poems, there appear, grouped under a heading of "Ignoto," three epigram-sonnets, attributed in Trinity College (Dublin) MS. F.4.20 to "Sr. Jo. Dauys"; and these mock in their coarse language the conventional attitudes and language of contemporary love poetry.[31] But in the so-called *Gulling Sonnets* Davies best demonstrates his skill in literary parody, as his "camelion Muse" assumes "divers shapes of gross absurdities" to ridicule the love sonnets of the 1590's.

The *Gulling Sonnets* consist of nine sonnets prefaced by a sonnet dedicating the series to Davies' "*good freinde Sr Anth. Cooke*," but little evidence exists for dating the composition of these poems. On the assumption that they were written near the time of the dedication, the limiting dates would be 1596–1604, the dates of Cooke's knighthood (following the English victory at Cadiz in which he participated) and Cooke's death. The *Sonnets* were not published until the nineteenth century, but, as with others of Davies' poems, they were probably circulated in manuscript.[32]

The distant example of Petrarch's love sonnets addressed to

Laura exerted a considerable influence, both directly and indirectly through other writers, on English poets in the last quarter of the sixteenth century. In these famous poems the great Italian poet and Humanist worshipfully extolled the physical and spiritual beauties of Laura and also analyzed the significance of her love and the various emotional states which it stimulated in him. Thomas Watson helped draw the attention of poets of Davies' generation to Petrarch's love poetry when he published in 1582 *Hekatompathia or Passionate Centurie of Love,* a collection of a hundred sonnets derived from Petrarch and other Continental poets.[33] Of greater influence in establishing the vogue of sonneteering in England, however, was Sir Philip Sidney's sonnet sequence *Astrophel and Stella,* written around 1581–1583 and first published in 1591. Sidney's fame as the Elizabethan courtier *par excellence* and the high poetic art exhibited in these sonnets attracted great attention to *Astrophel and Stella.* Circulated in manuscript before its publication, the cycle "shares with Spenser's *Shepheardes Calendar* the honor of inaugurating one of the greatest ages of English poetry."[34]

Following the publication of *Astrophel and Stella,* love sonnet-cycles became exceedingly popular. Among those by major poets are Samuel Daniel's *Delia* (1593); Michael Drayton's *Idea's Mirror* (1594); and Edmund Spenser's *Amoretti,* published along with his great marriage poem *Epithalamion* (1595). Although Shakespeare's sonnets were not published until 1609, it is probable that most were written during the 1590's. In addition to these major writers, a host of lesser talents, like Henry Constable, Bartholomew Griffin, William Smith, and Robert Tofte, contributed to the swell of love sonnets.[35]

First-rate poets adapt literary conventions to their own purposes and thereby achieve originality within the tradition and, at the same time, add a resonance to their poems; but less skillful poets sometimes merely repeat and baldly imitate, often bringing their work close to absurdity as they unimaginatively seek to emulate (or steal from) their betters. In such writers, the familiar themes of the love sonnet become deadening and mechanical, and the images and figures of speech appear hackneyed, or sometimes desperately ludicrous as the poet strives to disguise his commonplace ideas with verbal ingenuity.

"The pertinacity," as Sidney Lee observes, "with which the crude artificialities and plagiarisms of the sonnet sequence of love were cultivated in the last years of Queen Elizabeth's reign involved the sonnet as a form of poetic art in a storm of critical censure before the vogue expired."[36] One of Shakespeare's most popular sonnets cleverly turns on his rejection of the extravagant conceits and images of his fellow-sonneteers in favor of frank "russet yeas and honest kersey noes" in proclaiming his genuine love for a real, unliterary lady:

CXXX

My mistress's eyes are nothing like the sun;
Coral is far more red than her lips' red;
If snow be white, why then her breasts are dun;
If hairs be wires, black wires grow on her head.
I have seen roses damask'd, red and white,
But no such roses see I in her cheeks;
And in some perfumes is there more delight
Than in the breath that from my mistress reeks.
I love to hear her speak, yet well I know
That music hath a far more pleasing sound;
I grant I never saw a goddess go;
My mistress, when she walks, treads on the ground,
   And yet, by heaven, I think my love as rare
   As any she beli'd with false compare.

More caustic and heavy-fisted mockery of the love sonnets can be found in Joseph Hall's *Virgidemiarum* (1597). Hall ridicules the excessive idealization of the ladies and jeers at the routine attitudes and unfelt language of the sonneteers.[37]

As Davies makes clear in his dedication to Cooke, sonnet-writers are his targets in the *Gulling Sonnets*:

Here My Camelion Muse her selfe doth chaunge
to diuers shapes of gross absurdities
and like an Antick mocks wth fashion straunge
the fond admirers of lewde gulleries.
Your iudgement sees wth pitty, and wth scorne
The bastard Sonnetts of these Rymers bace,
W^{ch} in this whiskinge age are daily borne
To their owne shames, and Poetrie's disgrace.

Parody involves the distortion of a writer's style or habit of thought, sometimes by exaggerating salient features of his style or by drawing remote, low, or disgusting consequences or implications from the writer's characteristic ideas and attitudes. These techniques can be found in the *Gulling Sonnets* as Davies makes fun of the pretentious technique and stereotyped attitudes found in some Renaissance love poetry.

In sonnets 1 and 2 familiar attitudes and ideas of the sonneteers are made ridiculous by the remote and unexpected consequences which Davies draws from them. In Sonnet 1, the lover has so suffered under the burden of his mistress's love and has borne it so patiently that "the heav'nes at length to pity his distresse," transform him, appropriately enough, into "a patiente burden-bearinge Asse." In the second sonnet, Davies draws an analogy between the power of a single thought of the "poysonous beauty" of a lover to affect the lover's whole state of being and that of a single sheep to spread scurvy in a disgusting way throughout a whole flock. In sonnets 4 and 6, two fanciful extended figures of speech are debased by the addition of drably prosaic details as the analogy is elaborated. In Sonnet 4, because of the "hardness of her harte" and the "truth" of his, "the all seeinge eyes of heaven" "streight concluded" to turn her heart to flint; his, to steel. Between the two "sprange forthe the flame / of kindest love" which would have endured unendingly,

> Vntill my folly did her fury moue
> to recompence my seruice wth despighte,
> and to put out wth snuffers of her pride
> the lampe of loue wch els had neuer dyed.

In Sonnet 6, Davies clothes the god of love, "naked and without attyre," with symbolic garments of a sixteenth-century gentleman:

> The sacred Muse that firste made loue deuine
> hath made him naked and w^thout attyre,
> but I will cloth him wth this penn of myne
> that all the world his fashion shall admyre.
> his hatt of hope, his bande of beautye fine,

> his cloake of crafte, his doblett of desyre,
> greife for a girdell, shall aboute him twyne,
> his pointes of pride, his Ilet holes of yre,
> his hose of hate, his Cod peece of conceite,
> his stockings of sterne strife, his shirte of shame;
> his garters of vaine glorie gaye and slyte;
> his pantofels of passions I will frame,
> pumpes of presumption shall adorne his feete
> and Socks of sullennes excedinge sweete.

Among collections of epigrams, epitaphs, sonnets, and other minor verse of the sixteenth century, we encounter various forms of word-play and verbal ingenuities. Anagrams; chronograms, in which capital letters refer to some significant date; palindromes, words, phrases, or sentences which letter for letter read the same forward or backward; *verses recurrentes*, verses which, read forward, give one meaning—backward, another; various forms of correlative verse; and verses written in the shapes of pyramids and wings are among the verbal skill-games engaged in.[38] Davies satirizes such gulling wit in sonnets 3 and 5.

In sonnet 3, the rhetorical device of *reduplicatio*, in which the last word or words of one unit are repeated at the beginning of the next, is parodied. Perhaps in addition to ridiculing a stylistic device, the sonnet also mocks the tendency of poor poets to let the repetition of stock words substitute for a genuine advance or development of thought. The opening lines of Sonnet 3 make clear the kind of rhetorical abuse Davies is ridiculing:

> What Eagle can behould her sunbrighte eye,
> her sunbrighte eye y^t lights the world wth loue,
> the world of Loue wherin I liue and dye,
> I liue and dye and diuers chaunges proue,
> I chaunges proue, yet still the same am I,
> the same am I and neuer will remoue. . . .

Sonnet 5 satirizes a form of pattern or "trick" poetry known as correlative or reporting verse. In some forms of such verse, words or phrases of the first half of a line are meant to correlate with units in the second half; in others, phrase units are so arranged that they may be read horizontally or vertically—and usually with about the same lack of distinction either way. While major poets like Spenser and Milton adapted techniques of correlative verse with pleasing effect,[39] in other writers the surface cleverness distracts from and distorts the poem's effectiveness, producing a kind of verbal freak. A well-known example of such correlative verse, sometimes attributed to Sir Walter Raleigh, appears in *The Phoenix Nest* (1593), and reads:

Hir face,	Hir tong,	Hir wit,
So faire,	So sweete,	So sharpe,
First bent,	Then drew,	Then hit,
Mine eie,	Mine eare,	My hart.

Mine eie,	Mine eare,	My hart,
To like,	To learne,	To loue,
Hir face,	Hir tong,	Hir wit,
Doth lead,	doth teach,	Doth moue.

Oh face,	Oh tong,	Oh wit,
With frownes,	With checke,	With smart,
Wrong not,	Vexe not,	Wound not,
Mine eie,	Mine eare,	My hart.

Mine eie,	Mine eare,	My hart,
To learne,	To knowe,	To feare,
Hir face,	Hir tong,	Hir wit,
Doth lead,	Doth teach,	Doth sweare.[40]

The first four lines of Davies' Sonnet 5 may be compared to the foregoing:

Myne Eye,	mine eare,	my will,	my witt,	my harte
did see,	did heare,	did like,	discerne,	did loue:
her face,	her speche,	her fashion,	iudgem^t,	arte,
wch did charme,	please,	delighte,	confounde	and moue.

It is difficult to distinguish the parody here from its subject, but it seems principally to involve an excessive use of correlative verse: instead of working in units of threes, Davies makes the device even more tedious by piling up units of five.

As P. Burwell Rogers has suggested,[41] the *Gulling Sonnets* seem primarily intended to satirize a widespread style of poetry rather than individual poets or recognized sonnet cycles. But sonnets 7, 8, and 9 feature a heavy use of legal conceits and jargon, and Sonnet 8 names "Zepheria" as the object of the poet's praise, which would seem to parody an anonymous sonnet sequence which was published in 1594. Entitled *Zepheria,* the sequence contains forty "Canzons" of varying length, many of which are remarkable for obscure neologisms and awkward phrasing and sentence structure. The following is a fairly typical example:

Canzon. 20

How often hath my pen mine hearts solicitour
Instructed thee in breuiat of my case?
While fancie pleading eyes (thy beauties visitour)
Haue patternd to my quill an angels face.
How haue my Sonnets (faithfull counsellers)
Thee without ceasing mou'd for day of hearing?
While they my plaintiue cause (my faiths reuealers)
Thy long delay, my patience in thine eare-ring.
How haue I stood at barre of thine owne conscience?
When in requesting court my suite I brought.
How haue thy long adiournments flow'd the sentence,
Which I through much expense of teares besought?
Through many difficulties haue I run,
Ah sooner wert thou lost (I wis) then wonne.[42]

Alongside such a piece, Davies' parody in his Sonnet 8 becomes clear:

My case is this, I love Zepheria brighte,
Of her I hold my harte by fealtye:
Wch I discharge to her perpetuallye,
Yet she thereof will neuer me acquite.
for now supposinge I wᵗʰhold her righte
she hathe distreinde my harte to satisfie
the duty wᶜʰ I neuer did denye,
and far away impounds it wᵗʰ despite;
I labor therefore iustlie to repleaue
my harte wᶜʰ she vniustly doth impounde

but quick conceite wch nowe is loue's highe Sheife
retornes it as esloynde, not to be founde:
Then wch the lawe affords I onely craue
her harte for myne in wit her name to haue.

Although the *Gulling Sonnets* have a limited appeal for most modern readers, requiring as they do a knowledge of their literary context for an appreciation of their subtleties, they have considerable interest for the student of late Elizabethan literature, both for their intrinsic wit and for their reflection of a significant change in literary taste. They suggest, too, that we find in Davies a sharp, critical mind which was broadly conversant with the poetry of his own day.

III   Ten Sonnets to Philomel

Davies scoffed at the verbal and emotional excesses of other sonneteers, but he also wrote a short sequence of love sonnets—and in so doing scarcely avoided the very excesses and overworked conceits which he had ridiculed in the *Gulling Sonnets*. Despite the fact that very little "love" poetry has been attributed to him, we might expect a young poet living in London in the 1590's on some literary occasion or other to have paled before his mistress, to have suffered the chills and fevers of cruel love, and to have moaned in "poore Petrarch's long deceased woes" about his anguish. Grosart prints a few love lyrics of minor charm and interest, such a "A fragment of a Love Elegie," "To His Lady-Love," "Elegies of Loue," "Love-Lines," and "Love-Flight."[43] But Davies' most significant venture in this mode of poetry is the *Ten Sonnets to Philomel*.

These sonnets were first printed in 1602 in *A Poetical Rhapsody*, where they were signed "Melophilus."[44] In the succeeding editions of the *Rhapsody*, 1608, 1611, and 1621, they were signed "I. D.," initials appended to other of Davies' poems included in the anthology. In his edition of Davies' poetry in The Fuller Worthies Library in 1869, A. B. Grosart excluded these sonnets, regarding them as the work of John Donne; but he later changed his mind about this attribution and admitted them to *The Complete Poems of Sir John Davies* in 1876.[45] Concluding an explanation for ascribing them to Davies, Grosart assured students of *Orchestra* and the *Hymnes of Astraea* that they would "readily see the 'fine Roman hand' that wrote them in the *Ten Sonnets to Philomel*."[46] Although the evidence concerning their authorship is by no means overpowering, what exists seems to support the attribution to Davies. Little is added to his poetic stature if they are his; little is lost should future research prove they are another's.

The ten sonnets, all in the "Shakespearean" pattern, develop familiar love themes, in familiar images and conceits. Sonnets I and II concern the lover's reactions to hearing about Philomel or, as the heading in I reads: *"Vpon loues entring by his Eares."* Hearing about "sweet Philomel" binds his heart "in fettering chaines of Loue," racking him "with hope and feare" (Sonnet I), and causing him to suffer "dreadfull feare" and anguish (Sonnet II). Sonnets III and IV also develop a common theme: "his Mistris sicknes at one time," possibly suggesting a reality to Philomel that the other sonnets hardly support. Sonnet V turns on the familiar comparison between the distressed lover and a ship at sea, and its uninspired ticking off of analogies would have offered a tempting target for the kind of parody involved in the sixth *Gulling Sonnet*. Sonnet VI is headed *"Vpon her looking secretly out of a window as hee passed by,"* and Sonnet VII develops in an almost grotesque way the image of the lover's heart inflamed by his passion:

> When time nor place would let me often view
>   Natures chiefe Mirror, and my sole delight;
>   Her liuely Picture in my hart I drew,
>   That I might it behold both day and night,
> But shee, like *Phillips* Son, scorning that I
>   Should portray her wanting *Apelles* Art,
>   Commaunded Loue (who nought dare hir deny)
>   To burne the Picture which was in my Hart.
> The more Loue burn'd the more her picture shin'd;
>   The more it shin'de, the more my hart did burne:
>   So what to hurt her picture was assign'd,
>   To my Harts ruine and decay did turne.
> Loue could not burne the Saint, it was diuine,
> And therefore fir'd my hart, the Saints poore shrine.

Sonnet VII likens his Love's power to dispel his "clouds of dispaire" to the glory and might of the sun. Sonnet IX, headed *"Vpon sending her a Gold Ring, with this Posie Pure, and Endlesse,"* finds similarities between his lady and gold, but also important differences:

> That whereas Gold the more tis purifi'd,
> By waxing lesse, doth shew some part is spent,
> My Loue doth wax more pure by you more trying,
> And yet encreaseth in the purifying.

The concluding sonnet records a rebuff by the lady and her recommendation that Melophilus apply his attentions elsewhere, to which the faithful lover replies with a complimentary analogy between the sun and his Philomel.

These sonnets are probably no worse than hundreds like them, but they bring little credit to their author. If they are Davies', they suggest that his true métier was the witty and lightly ironic verse of the *Epigrams* and *Orchestra* and the poetry of succinct and clearly articulated statement of *Nosce Teipsum*.

CHAPTER 3

In Praise of the Dance

DAVIES' most delightful and engaging poem, and probably his most interesting for the modern reader, is *Orchestra, or A Poeme of Dauncing. Iudicially prooving the true obseruation of time and measure, in the Authenticall and laudable vse of Dauncing.* Entered in the *Stationers' Register* in June, 1594,[1] it was first published in 1596 and reprinted, with revisions, in 1622. Davies could have been no more than twenty-five when he wrote "this suddaine, rash, half-capriole" of wit, which he dedicated "To his very Freind, Rich: Martin." In a prefatory sonnet, Davies credits his Temple companion in revels as the poem's "first mover and sole cause":

> To whom shall I this dancing poem send,
> This sudden, rash, half-capriole of my wit?
> To you, first mover and sole cause of it,
> Mine own self's better half, my dearest friend.
> Oh would you yet my Muse some honey lend
> From your mellifluous tongue, whereon doth sit
> Suada in majesty, that I may fit
> These harsh beginnings with a sweeter end.
> You know the modest sun full fifteen times
> Blushing did rise and blushing did descend
> While I, in making of these ill-made rimes,
> My golden hours unthriftily did spend.
> Yet, if in friendship you these numbers praise,
> I will mis-spend another fifteen days.[2]

Orchestra—a term which here preserves its ancient Greek meaning of dance—attracted the notice of Davies' contemporaries. Sir John Harington addressed an amusing, albeit somewhat indelicate epigram to Davies, who "the Planets all doe set to dancing."[3] Others mocked his elaborate encomium of dance: in *Lenten Stuffe* (1599), Thomas Nashe placed among certain frivolous writers one who "capers it up to the spheares in commendation of daunsing;"[4] and in *The Scourge of Villanie* (1598) John Marston ridiculed "spruce skipping Curio," declaring:

> Prayse but *Orchestra* and the skipping art
> You shall command him, faith you have his hart
> Even capring in your fist. A hall, a hall.
> Roome for the spheres, the Orbes celestiall
> We'll daunce *Kemps Jigge.* They'le revel with neate jumps
> A worthy Poet hath put on their Pumps.[5]

Davies' poem has enjoyed considerable favor in succeeding times, if only among a small and specially interested public. Described as "a graceful monument of ingenious fancy" (Arthur H. Bullen), "a clever *jeu d'esprit*" (F. E. Schelling), "the very spirit of gaiety" (Richard Lambert), a "coruscation of amorous enthusiasm" (Herbert Howarth), it has been praised for its "exquisite novelty" (Edmund Gosse), "happy exuberance" (Margarete Seemann), "poetical capers" (E. M. W. Tillyard), and sportive "playfulness" (G. A. Wilkes); these critical tags well indicate the essential qualities of the work, and the proper expectations with which to approach it.

I *Summary*

Orchestra consists of a fairly lengthy disputation concerning dance placed within a slight, and uncompleted, narrative frame. The opening stanzas (1–14) provide a context for the debate. In a pertly jocular manner, the poet explains that Homer, great as he was, had unfortunately forgotten to recount "The courtly love that Antinous did make" to the faithful Penelope, almost "as if it had not been." To remedy this oversight, he relates a discourse between the two. As her court assembles one evening at Ithaca, Antinous invites Penelope to dance; but she refuses, somewhat peevishly denigrating dancing as "this new rage" and calling it an instance of "disorder and misrule."

The major body of the poem (stanzas 15–118) treats Antinous' attempts to win his lady's consent by means of an elaborate apology for the dance. He insists that dancing is as old as the created universe and that its birth was almost simultaneous with Time, since "Time the measure of all moving is / And Dancing is a moving all in a measure." The ordered motions of dance are an expression of Love, that force which reduced the initial chaos to order; assigned the elements of fire, air, earth, and water their proper positions; and set the "starry wheels" of heaven spinning in "a well-ordered dance." Dancing is heaven's emblem, "heaven's true figure, and the earth's ornament."

Cautiously interested, Penelope questions how contemporary dancing, this "frantic jollity" Antinous would invite her to, relates to this ancient cosmic dance. Her wooer explains that Love, having set the universe dancing, turned his attention to mankind, whom he found "A rude disordered rout." Calling them into a ring about himself, Love alerted his audience to the presence of dance everywhere about them—in the movement of the stars, planets, elements; in the rhythmic motions of the sea, streams, flowers; and in the song and flight of the birds. The sun's motions are really those of a galliard; the moon's a pavan; and the stream's "indented course and wriggling play," "a perfect cunning hay." Dance can be seen in the most unlikely phenomena. Sound, for example, is really a dancing of the air,

> For, when you breathe the air in order moves
> Now in now out, in time and measure true;
> And when you speak, so well she dancing loves
> That doubling oft and oft redoubling new
> With thousand forms she doth herself endue:
> For all the words that from your lips repair
> Are nought but tricks and turnings of the air.   (St. 44)

"Sweet music," "dancing's only life," is born "when the air doth dance her finest measure." The rhythmic motions of streams, of flowers waving in the wind, of birds singing and flying are clearly forms of dance:

> For those blue veins that through her body spread,
> Those sapphire streams which from great hills do spring,

(The earth's great dugs, for every wight is fed
With sweet fresh moisture from them issuing)
Observe a dance in their wild wandering;
And still their dance begets a murmur sweet,
And still the murmur with the dance doth meet.   (St. 52)

* * *

See how those flowers, that have sweet beauty too,
(The only jewels that the earth doth wear,
When the young sun in bravery her doth woo)
As oft as they the whistling wind do hear,
Do wave their tender bodies here and there;
And though their dance no perfect measure is,
Yet oftentimes their music makes them kiss.   (St. 55)

* * *

Hark how the birds do sing and mark then how,
Jump with the modulation of their lays,
They lightly leap and skip from bough to bough.
Yet do the cranes deserve a greater praise,
Which keep such measure in their airy ways
As when they all in order ranked are
They make a perfect form triangular.   (St. 57)

Love's lecture won his audience's approbation, and their intent
looks indicated "That they would learn to dance, if Love would
teach." Love complied, teaching them first the seven motions
found in nature: "Upward and downward, forth and back
again, / To this side and to that, and turning round," (St. 62),
out of which he formed "a thousand brawls," "rounds and winding hays," and then "more grave and solemn measures." As his
students' proficiency grew, Love instructed them in the galliard,
"A swift and wand'ring dance" "With passages, uncertain, to and
fro," "With lofty turns and caprioles in the air"; in corantos
"That on a triple dactyl foot do run / Close by the ground with
sliding passages"; and lavoltas,

. . . the most delightful kind,
A lofty jumping, or a leaping round,
When arm in arm two dancers are entwin'd

And whirl themselves with strict embracements bound,
And still their feet an anapest do sound;
An anapest is all their music's song,
Whose first two feet are short and third is long.   (St. 70)

Under Love's tutelage, men learned "Sweet music's sound with feet to counterfeit" and dancing became a part of—perhaps a condition for—social observances and rituals,

... all ceremonious mysteries,
All sacred orgies and religious rites,
All pomps and triumphs and solemnities,
All funerals nuptials and like public sights,
All parliaments of peace and warlike fights,
All learned arts and every great affair,
A lively shape of dancing seems to bear.   (St. 77)

Unconvinced, Penelope counters that Love is "Of every ill the hateful father vile" and that the dance is something associated with "vainness, frenzy, and misorder." But Antinous distinguishes between Love and lust, and he appeals to his would-be lady to find the Love he speaks of within herself, for "true Love" dances galliards in her amorous eyes, and,

Love in the twinkling of your eyelids danceth,
Love danceth in your pulses and your veins,
Love, when you sew, your needle's point advanceth
And makes it dance a thousand curious strains
Of winding rounds, whereof the form remains,
To show that your fair hands can dance the hay,
Which your fine feet would learn as well as they.   (St. 106)

More importantly, Penelope's soul reflects the presence of dance,

Yet your fair soul, which came from heaven above
To rule this house (another heaven below),
With divers powers in harmony doth move;
And all the virtues that from her do flow
In a round measure hand in hand do go;
Could I now see, as I conceive, this dance,
Wonder and love would cast me in a trance.   (St. 108)

Sensing failure even after so earnest and arduous a dissertation, Antinous invokes the aid of Love, who intervenes and places in Penelope's hands a magic mirror which reveals the past, present, and future. As she gazes at her reflection, an image of a future time, a "golden age," begins to appear—in fact, a dazzling vision of Elizabeth's court where courtiers pay honor to their sovereign like "A thousand sparkling stars" shining about the "bright moon." The poet invokes the aid of Urania to inspire him with gifts like those of the great English poets and to move his mind with "such sacred fury" that he may be able to depict this vision of courtly dance. At this climactic moment in the 1596 version, the poem concludes—or, more accurately, stops.

II *The Question of the Poem's Ending*

The ending of the poem poses some critical problems. A. H. Bullen, who remarked that we need not regret Davies' failure to complete *Orchestra*, suggested that the poet would probably have given us more of the same, more variations on the theme of dance.[6] Perhaps so. Perhaps, too, a curiosity to know "how it all came out" may be inappropriate to what Davies thought he was attempting in *Orchestra*: writing a light, jesting, witty amplification of an idea. Performing a series of agile verbal acrobatics, all the more entertaining because executed on so slender a thematic rope and done with a gentlemanly "recklessnesse," Davies was unconcerned about such a fussy matter as formal symmetry.

We might regard the poem as an extended "invitation" or "courting" poem in which the focus is on the cleverness of the entreaty itself rather than on its ultimate success. In Marlowe's "Come Live With Me," for example, interest in whether the shepherdess does or does not accept the shepherd's invitation is displaced by the evocation of a joyful, carefree life, where "Melodious birds sing madrigals" and "shepherds' swains dance and sing each May morning." And in more sophisticated poems of amorous casuistry, like Donne's "The Ecstasy" or Marvell's "To His Coy Mistress," we find the wooer's witty exploitation of arcane knowledge or the relentless application of the syllogism toward sexual rewards sufficient justification for the poems.

Unfortunately, Davies develops the narrative frame just enough and so closely integrates the dance debate with it that the poem's inconclusive ending is disappointing. In addition, after so urgently invoking Urania's assistance, Davies' failure to produce the climactic vision of Elizabeth's court leaves the reader unfulfilled, like one whose Paris holiday has been suddenly cancelled.

Speculation about Davies' failure to complete *Orchestra* has not been very productive. Margarete Seeman has offered two possible, but unconvincing, explanations: one, Martin may not have praised the poem enough to encourage Davies to "mispend another fifteen days" in completing it; second, Davies may have been deterred by the satiric jibes of his contemporaries.[7] More recently, and more interestingly, Herbert Howarth has contended that the poem posed irresolvable problems for the poet. On one level, Davies' handling of the legend produced a contradiction difficult to reconcile in that Penelope, traditionally identified with marital fidelity, is besieged by the traditionally usurping Antinous' employing charmingly the venerable ideas of order and harmony to invite her to an act, symbolically at least, which would "spell a breach of the holy order of marriage." Beneath the fiction, Howarth maintains, is an even more profound contradiction for Davies and for his age: one between the concept of a world as limited and statically ordered and the observable realities of dynamic change.[8] But we wonder if a youthful Davies took his poem as seriously as such views imply. Perhaps he simply had had his fun with an idea; had amused others with his graceful wit; and, when his muse failed to bring "These harsh beginnings" to "a sweeter end," had moved on to other poems and interests.

Whatever Davies' reasons for not completing the poem, some indication of his likely intentions concerning its conclusion may be discerned in revisions which he made when *Orchestra* was republished, along with *Nosce Teipsum* and *Hymnes of Astraea* in 1622. Here the poem bears the subtitle "A poem expressing the antiquity and excellence of dancing, in a dialogue between Penelope and one of her wooers; not finished." In addition to minor changes in the 1596 text, Davies replaced the dedication to Martin with one to Prince Charles and omitted stanzas 127–

131, in which he invoked the aid of poets, among whom Martin is included.[9] Following stanza 126, he added: "*Here are wanting some stanzas describing Queen Elizabeth. Then follow these,*" five stanzas describing the "barons brave and ladies fair" dancing before Elizabeth, and Penelope's growing delight in the splendid vision. In his edition of the poem, Professor Tillyard suggests that these stanzas were part of the original poem and that they indicate Davies' original intention. Had he completed the poem, this vision of Elizabeth and her court would have persuaded Penelope to yield to Antinous' invitation to join him in dance, thereby bringing the elaborate entreaty to a happy conclusion.[10]

But to complement such views, notice should be taken of Robert Krueger's recent important suggestions concerning the poem's ending.[11] Because his argument is technical and closely reasoned, the reader should consult the original essay, but Krueger's principal contentions may be summarized here. Bodleian Library Add. MS. B.97, a commonplace-book of Leweston Fitzjames, a student with Davies at the Temple, preserves a number of Davies' poems, including the only known extant manuscript text of *Orchestra* (fols. 25–38). From the external evidence of the manuscript and the internal evidence of the poem, Krueger argues that the manuscript text is an earlier draft of the 1596 text and, in all probability, was transcribed from Davies' own draft in 1595 or 1596.

Krueger argues that the poem originally contained only 113 stanzas, 1–108 followed by 127–131 (the invocations), and that stanzas 109–126 were added later. His analysis of the physical make-up of the manuscript supports his argument. True, too, in terms of the poem's thematic development, as he contends, stanzas 109–126—which treat Concord, Comeliness, and Reason and recount the mirror incident—do seem to move away from the subject of dancing and focus on Penelope. Krueger suggests that Davies added these lines as an afterthought, either simply to compliment Elizabeth or to adapt the poem to an entertainment at which the monarch was present. He also suggests that the poem might have been "performed" as a debate which concluded with a tribute to Elizabeth and her assembled court.[12]

Krueger does not accept the validity of Tillyard's views concerning the change in the dedication made in the 1622 edition. He believes that the animosity which had led Davies to attack Martin lingered on; and, wishing to disassociate the poem entirely from his former friend, Davies replaced the dedicatory sonnet. In addition,

In order to remove his reference to the "Swallow" [an allusion to Martin] in the closing stanzas without this removal calling attention to his motive, he wrote five new stanzas which continue the description of Queen Elizabeth and her court but do not conclude the poem. He further concealed his removal of the stanzas to Martin with a false apology following stanza 126, "Here are wanting some stanzas describing Queen Elizabeth," and supported this fabrication with that of the title-page claiming the poem was "not finished."[13]

While Krueger's arguments require a good bit of hypothesizing and conjecturing, his conclusions seem reasonable and responsible. We should note, however, that in no version can the poem be said to be finished; the effect of Antinous' argument is never made known, and the poem ends with Penelope's decision undetermined.

III   Contexts and Sources

Tillyard wisely selected *Orchestra* as a typical Elizabethan poem in *Five Poems, 1470–1870*, a study of poems chosen to reflect the historical periods of their composition.[14] *Orchestra* is very much a part of the cultural context of late sixteenth-century England, and it interestingly mirrors the times in which it was written.

Several suggestions have been proffered concerning the literary context within which *Orchestra* should be considered. As an amatory tale of Classical legend or mythology, the poem seems related to the Ovidian or mythological narrative poem popular during the 1590's.[15] In such narratives as Thomas Lodge's *Scillaes Metamorphosis* (1589), Christopher Marlowe's *Hero and Leander* (1593?), Shakespeare's *Venus and Adonis* (1593), and others, mythological love stories are retold, richly decorated with pictorial imagery and rhetorical ornament. In addition, the narrative frequently serves as an excuse for the discussion of, or comment upon, thoughtful matters, as in *Venus and Adonis* where the titular figures engage in a debate concerning sexual gratification and sexual purity.[16]

While *Orchestra* is not so lushly pictorial as such poems and while it substitutes a more cerebral wittiness for their erotic appeal, its treatment of Classical legend and the courting situation of Antinous and Penelope invite comparison. However, David Daiches suggests another perspective on the poem by regarding it as an example of the "educational and philosophic verse" written by such poets as Fulke Greville, George Chapman, and Samuel Daniel.[17] The philosophical implications of Antinous' views and the poet's apparent erudition perhaps recall such poets' work, but Davies' gay tone and the lambent humor that play about Antinous' dissertation set *Orchestra* apart from the discursive poems of these more solemn philosophers in verse.

The playful, really mock-learned tone of the poem is, in fact, so important a characterizing element as to suggest parody or intellectual burlesque rather than serious philosophical exposition. The disproportion between Antinous' rigorous argument supported by learnedly developed evidence and the comparatively trivial end it seeks—a dance with Penelope—generates a quality analogous to the play of form against matter found in mock-epics such as Drayton's *Nymphidia* and Pope's *The Rape of the Lock*. Davies' facetious encomium of dance is similar to the intellectual spoofing we find in the mock-learned dissertations which were sometimes a part of the "solemn foolery" of the law students' revels.[18]

Philip J. Finkelpearl, who has also noted such a quality about *Orchestra*, describes the poem's dominant effect as "one of calculated and extended wittiness of the sort which occurs frequently in quasi-academic 'defenses' and in such genres as the paradox and the problem."[19] Building on Krueger's hypothesis that *Orchestra* might actually have been presented before some courtly audience, Finkelpearl suggests that it may well have been "performed" during the revels at the Middle Temple in 1597–98 with Richard Martin, who served as the leader of these festivities, reciting the lines assigned to "Love."[20] Such a speculation is purely hypothetical, but the tone of *Orchestra* and its amusingly learned wit would certainly be appropriate to such a Saturnalian occasion and audience.

Perhaps the category to which *Orchestra* can best be related is that described by Northrop Frye as "Menippean" satire or "anatomy." In its shorter form, Frye explains, Menippean satire "is usually a dialogue or colloquy, in which the dramatic interest is in a conflict of ideas rather than of character."[21] In dealing with such intellectual themes, the writer "shows his exuberance in intellectual ways, by piling up an enormous mass of erudition about his theme...."[22] Frye finds manifestations of "this creative treatment of exhaustive erudition" to be the organizing principle of Robert Burton's massive *Anatomy of Melancholy,* in which human society is minutely studied in terms of the concept of melancholy. The word "anatomy" in Burton's title meant a dissection or analysis, and it suggests the elaborate divisions and subdivisions into which he partitions his principal subject and the copious illustrations which he gives for each.[23]

This kind of organizing principle is also present in a work like Erasmus' *The Praise of Folly* in which "folly" is the controlling concept which the Dutch Humanist illustrates with numerous examples; in the section in Montaigne's *An Apology for Raymond Sebond* in which the essayist catalogues example after example of the manifest superiority of animals to mankind; and in Donne's first *Paradox*, "A Defense of Women's Inconstancy," in which the poet ironically defends feminine inconstancy by a host of ingenious reasons. It is interesting that John Hoskins, one of Davies' associates at the Middle Temple, cited *Orchestra* in his work on rhetoric, *Directions for Speech and Style*, as an example of the rhetorical device of "Division" or "Anatomie."[24]

Davies may claim as his own the witty execution and elaboration of the poem, but the principal ideas of *Orchestra*, especially the symbolic treatment of dance and the Empedoclean concept of Love as the ordering and harmonizing creative force in the universe, as Tillyard has indicated, come from "the accumulated doctrines of many years."[25] Dance as a metaphor for cosmic order can be found as early as Plato's *Timaeus*:

The earth, which is our nurse, clinging around the pole which is extended through the universe, he framed to be the guardian and artificer of night and day, first and eldest of gods that are in the interior of heaven. Vain would be the attempt to tell all the figures of them circling as in dance, and their juxtapositions, and the return of them in their revolutions upon themselves. . . .[26]

This idea is not unfamiliar in later times. Varro, for example, observed: "That round dance of the stars, the positions of the planets in relation to the fixed stars, the beautiful order and perfect harmony in all their movements—what is all that if not a picture of a primeval dance!"[27] Syneseos of Cyrene spoke of the stars as "the dancing company that encircles the universe,"[28] and elsewhere praised God, under whose direction "the seven planets dance in harmony in the powerful revolutions of the great vault. . . ."[29] Moreover, astral dance imagery figures also in Renaissance writers besides Davies. Du Bartas employs such imagery in his popular epic, *Divine Weeks and Works,* Montaigne in his *Essays,* and Milton in several of his poems.[30] In addition to such literary examples, dance is treated as a metaphor of cosmic order in the choreography of the courtly masques in Davies' time, both in France and in England.

Frances A. Yates has discussed the speculations of Antoine de Baïf and his colleagues in the French academies concerning dance and its almost mystical capacity to harmonize participants and spectators and to bring them into rapport with their universe, and shown how such notions were incorporated in the *Ballet Comique de la Reine,* performed for a court wedding in 1581.[31] John C. Meagher has discussed the symbolic significance which Ben Jonson attached to dance as an image of cosmic order, of the motion of the elements, and of the seasons in such masques as *The Masque of Beauty, Love Restored, Pleasure Reconciled to Vertue,* and *The Vision of Delight.*[32] Although the symbolic function of the dance is more implicit in Shakespeare's plays than in Jonson's masques, J. R. Brown has shown how Shakespeare employs dancing in his romantic comedies as emblems of social concord and harmony.[33]

Thus, Davies in writing *Orchestra* was drawing upon a store of ideas and a way of thought centuries old and perhaps almost as traditional and as familiar as the metaphors we use unconsciously in our everyday conversation. But, to stimulate his wit and to aid him in his anatomizing of the dance, Davies turned to one of the most prominent Classical treatises on dancing. A. H. Bullen seems first to have noted the parallels in idea and incidental details between *Orchestra* and Lucian's *Peri Orkheseos*, a dialogue between Crato, who castigates dancing, and Lycinus, who praises and wittily defends it against a number of aspersions.[34] Dance as a metaphor of cosmic order, the ancient origin of dance, the Empedoclean concept of Love all clearly appear in this dialogue; and they do so in formulations very reminiscent of *Orchestra*. Lucian writes, for example, about the origin of dance: "Those historians of dancing who are the most veracious can tell you that Dance comes into being contemporaneously with the primal origin of the universe, making her appearance together with Love—the love that is age-old. In fact, the concord of the heavenly spheres, the interlacing of the errant planets with the fixed stars, their rhythmic agreement and timed harmony, are proof that Dance was primordial."[35]

Davies seems to have helped himself to details from Lucian's dialogue, as can be seen by comparing the following passages:

Even the Indians, when they get up in the morning and pray to the sun, instead of doing as we do, who think that when we have kissed our hand the prayer is complete, face the sunrise and welcome the God of Day with dancing, posturing in silence and imitating the dance of the god; and that, to the Indians, is prayer and dance and sacrifice all in one. So they propitiate their god with those rites twice each day, when it begins and when it declines.[36]

¤   ¤   ¤

As, when the Indians, neighbours of the morning,
In honour of the cheerful rising sun,
With pearl and painted plumes themselves adorning,
A solemn stately measure have begun;
The god, well-pleas'd with that fair honour done,
Shines forth his beams, and doth their faces kiss
With that immortal glorious face of his:

(St. 136)

¤   ¤   ¤

For it seems to me that the ancient myth about Proteus the Eygptian means nothing else than that he was a dancer, an imitative fellow, able to shape himself and change himself into anything, so that he could imitate even the liquidity of water and the sharpness of fire in the liveliness of his movement; yes, the fierceness of a lion, the rage of a leopard, the quivering of a tree, and in a word whatever he wished.[37]

○   ○   ○

> Wherefore was Proteus said himself to change
> Into a stream a lion and a tree,
> And many other forms fantastic strange,
> As in his fickle thought he wish'd to be?
> But that he danc'd with such facility,
> As like a lion he could pace with pride,
> Ply like a plant, and like a river slide.   (St. 81)

In addition to indebtedness to Lucian, Davies in his fanciful treatment of the dance owes something to Sir Thomas Elyot's *The Boke Named the Gouernour* (1531), a central and popular Humanist work.[38] In this treatise on the education of young nobility, Elyot devotes a number of chapters to dancing as a proper and useful exercise in the education of a courtier.[39] Drawing on Lucian and on a number of early writers, Elyot rehearses notions of the origin of dance at the time of creation and reviews its subsequent history and the importance attached to dancing in Classical times.

Climaxing his discussion, Elyot "moralizes" the dance; he turns it into an elaborate allegory in which the steps, movements, and gestures can be construed in conceptual terms. In as ingenious a bit of analogizing as can be found in Davies' *Orchestra*, Elyot shows how the eight steps of the *basse danse* can be interpreted as lessons about "the first morall vertue, called prudence." Dancing affords not only healthful exercise; it can serve as a pleasant introduction to the study of such virtues as industry, circumspection, modesty, and prudence. Elyot's soberly pedagogical dissertation contrasts sharply with the gay, jocular banter of *Orchestra*, and there is a reversal in figurative tenor and vehicle in the two writers: for Elyot, the dance is a vehicle bearing significant meanings for conduct; for Davies, natural phenomena and images of human activity are vehicles for dance. But Elyot's allegorizing mode of thought and ingenious analogizing are not far removed from Davies' essential method in *Orchestra*.

Mention might be made here, too, of an anticipation of Davies' poem, Bérenger de La Tour's *Choreïde, Autrement, Lovenge du Bal*, published at Lyon in 1556. La Tour (1522?-1599?) was a lawyer and a poet.[40] *Choreïde* is a charming poem, a monologue of 324 lines in octosyllabic couplets, dedicated in a jocular way to the instruction of several ladies. Opening the poem with a formal statement of subject and with an invocation to the Muses, La Tour, drawing on Lucian, reviews the ancient origin of dance, finding it coeval with the motions of the planets; and he notes its manifestation in the play of the flames, the motion of the sea, and the fluttering of the leaves in the wind. The tone throughout is light and playful, quite like Davies' in *Orchestra*. Similarities in basic ideas and details are probably best explained by the two poets' drawing upon a common source; but it is tempting to speculate that Davies—or Martin, whom he credited as the poem's "first mover and cause"—came across *Choreïde* during the visit to the Continent in 1592 and found its gay, clever poetic treatment of dancing a precedent for his more elaborately developed apology.

The Platonism of *Orchestra* is also a reflection of intellectual concerns of sixteenth-century England. In stanzas 102–108, as Tillyard has shown,[41] appear ideas of physical and spiritual love and beauty and their meaningful relationship which represent fairly common topics in Elizabethan thought. Davies may well have known Castiglione's popular and influential courtesy book, *The Courtier*, with its lengthy discourse on Platonic love by Cardinal Bembo in Book IV, as well as Spenser's *Four Hymns* (1596), a work which celebrates earthly and heavenly love and beauty. But Davies hardly needed a "source" for such ideas; they were among the intellectual inventory of many of his educated contemporaries and, as Rosamond Tuve has said, were the intellectual commonplaces of the day.[42]

Not to swamp the delicate charm of *Orchestra* with too much consideration of context, one further relationship to its historical period should be noted, for I believe it places Davies' witty performance in clearer relief. As suggested by its subtitle in the 1622 edition—"A poem expressing the antiquity and excellency of dancing"—*Orchestra* seems to have some reference to the debate over dancing which went on during the sixteenth and seventeenth centuries.[43] Despite glorious accomplishments during these centuries, the arts were frequently on the defensive against a host of critics. Like music, literature, and drama, dance sustained attacks by moralists who feared it would lead the young and pliable into paths of iniquity. As an enticement of the Devil, dancing was denounced by a host of writers, both on the Continent and in England; and the bibliography of such criticism is large and usually intensely vehement. The following passages from Philip Stubbes' *Anatomy of Abuses* (1583) are fairly indicative of both the tone and the substance of the animadversions upon dancing:

Dauncing, as it is vsed (or rather abused) in these daies, is an introduction to whordom, a preparatiue to wantonnes, a prouocatiue to vncleanes, & an introite to al kind of lewdenes, rather than a pleasant exercyse to *the* mind, or a holsome practise for *the* body: yet, notwithstanding, . . . both men, wemen, & children, are so skilful in this laudable science, as they maye be thought nothing inferiour to *Cynoedus, the* prostitut ribauld, nor yet to *Sardanapalus,* that effeminat varlet. Yea, thei are not ashamed to erect scholes of dauncing, thinking it an ornament to their children to be expert in this noble science of heathen diuelrie: and yet this people glory of their christianitie & integritie of life.

⁕ ⁕ ⁕

For what clipping, what culling, what kissing and bussing, what smouching & slabbering one of another, what filthie groping and vncleane handling is not practised euery wher in these dauncings? yea, the very deed and action it selfe, which I will not name for offending chast eares, shall be purtrayed and shewed foorth in their bawdye gestures of one to another. All which, whither they blow vp *Venus* cole or not, who is so blind that seeth not? wherefore, let them not think that it is any recreation . . . to the mind of a good Christian, but rather a corrosiue most sharp and nipping. . . . And wheras they conclude it is a holesome exercise for the bodie, the contrary is moste true; for I haue knowen diuers, by the immoderate vse therof, haue in short time become decrepit and lame, so remaining to their dying day. Some haue broke their legs with skipping, leaping, turning, and vawting, and some haue come by one hurt, some by another, but neuer any come from thence without someparte of his minde broken and lame; such a wholesome exercise it is! But, say they, it induceth looue: so I say also; but what looue? Truely, a lustful loue, a venereous looue, a concupiscencious, baudie, & beastiall looue, such as proceedeth from the stinking pump and lothsome sink of Carnall affection and fleshly appetite, and not such as distilleth from the bowels of the hart inginerat by the spirit of God.[44]

But dancing had its defenders. Some were teachers of dance like Thoinot Arbeau;[45] some, like Elyot, Roger Ascham, and Richard Mulcaster,[46] headmaster of Merchant Taylors' School, were humanists and educators who saw dancing as a useful social grace for a young man to have. Perhaps even more sturdy support came from the great popularity dancing enjoyed among the citizenry and especially in courtly circles. Elizabeth was an expert dancer herself, and many of the entertainments at court involved various kinds of dancing.[47] It is not impossible that Davies, youthful and pleasure loving, registered his displeasure with such strait-laced, nay-saying moralists as Philip Stubbes, Stephen Gosson, and John Northbrook by writing so extravagantly and almost impishly in praise of dance. Certainly, against the gloomy and stormy denunciations of such austere critics, Davies' amusingly graceful encomium appears in refreshing and bright relief.

IV   Orchestra *and the Theme of World Order*

"If we consider the nature of the subject," wrote Alexander Chalmers in 1810, *Orchestra* "is a wonderful instance of what a man of genius may elicit from trifles."[48] In the years since this statement, students have found much more in the poem than the superficial trifles which struck Chalmers. Its real subject, as C. S. Lewis noted, is " 'all the choir of heaven and all the furniture of earth.' "[49] The conceits of its stanzas comprise a world view, one fundamentally different from ours, however many of its elements linger on unexamined in our assumptions about life and our relationship to it.

The refractions of the "enchanted glass" through which thoughtful men of the Renaissance viewed the universe have been studied by a number of eminent scholars,[50] and they seem to be in basic agreement about the essential characteristics of that perspective. "The Elizabethan World Picture" is, however, under attack these days. Some think any broad generalizations about a complex era are over-simplifications and inescapable distortions,[51] but certain elements of the Elizabethan world view that are substantiated by contemporary evidence justify consideration and, if used with caution, offer us useful insights into the literature of the period.

In brief terms, one of the essential elements of this world view is a purposive, significant, and knowable order in the universe—an order to which the multifarious data of the cosmos, earth, human society, and the individual can be related. Tillyard has noted three principal figures by which this organization was imaged in Renaissance thought.[52] One was a chain of being, which extended from the throne of God to the least part of inanimate matter, an image suggesting a distinct hierarchy in the gradations of being which it represented. In the chain, man occupied a difficult middle position between the lowest rank of angels and the highest forms of animal life; and wisdom lay in a man's knowing his place and in his finding what satisfaction he could in it. Within categories there were other gradations: kings were higher beings than their subjects; husbands, than their wives.

A second figure was that of a series of parallel planes with interconnecting correspondences. The orderly disposition of the angelic hosts assembled around the throne of God was a meaningful pattern for the orderly structure of a political state with its prince at the center and his advisors and subjects arranged about him, and the political state served as a pattern for the proper ordering of an individual with his passions carefully kept in check by his Will under the direction of his Wit. The validity of such conceptions was reenforced by the number of correspondences which could be discerned between the larger and "the little world of man." Some solace was to be had from the recognition, for example, of numerical analogies: the seven ages of man and the seven planets, the four elements of matter and the four physiological "humors" composing man.[53] While there were those who scoffed at astrology, the notion of a planetary influence upon human life fitted neatly into such a scheme of thought in that it suggested a significant connection between one plane and another.

A third image of world order noted by Tillyard was the dance, not exclusively, as we have seen, but most thoroughly and delightfully developed in Davies' poem. Dance as an emblem of order is perhaps related to similar interpretations of music. The harmonies of music seemed fit metaphors for the harmony of the soul, and the ancient notion of the music of the spheres served as a symbol of cosmic harmony and concord. Davies developed ideas such as these in his "A Hymne in Prayse of Musicke."[54] As a symbol of order, dance accommodated motion in the otherwise static views of the world as a chain or as a series of related planes of being. In a dance, the participants' positions and movements, rhythms and tempos, are subordinated to the dance; and all participants are related to each other through the dance. By analogy, all creatures and nature can be seen to move, as it were, in an orderly dance of life—a dance whose rhythms and movements are under the direction of God. The Concord of social life shines forth as in a gay dance,

> Where divers men and women ranked be,
> And every one doth dance a several part,
> Yet all as one in measure do agree,
> Observing perfect uniformity;
> All turn together, all together trace,
> And all together honour and embrace.   (St. 110)

And "Comeliness, the child of Order sweet," is properly pictured as a dance:

> For Comeliness is a disposing fair
> Of things and actions in fit time and place,
> Which doth in dancing show itself most clear,
> When troops confus'd, which here and there do trace
> Without distinguishment or bounded space,
> By dancing rule into such ranks are brought
> As glads the eye and ravisheth the thought.   (St. 114)

As Tillyard notes,[55] Davies' development of the dance image throughout the poem also implies the figures of the chain of being and the scheme of correspondences. Antinous ranges throughout all creation and time, from the motions of the heavenly bodies to matters terrestrial to the light dancing in Penelope's eyes and the virtues in her soul. And the dances on the various planes of being have significances for Antinous' lady: they become justifications for her participating in the dance, and they suggest that her refusal to do so is unnatural. The sparkling images and the well-turned rhyme royal stanzas, thus, turn back upon themselves and depict together a whole view of nature.

Tillyard's studies of the Elizabethan world view have attracted renewed interest in *Orchestra* in recent years, for he has used the poem as his principal example of the dance as a figure for world order.[56] While he was by no means insensitive to the poem as a poem and did not squeeze it to death in extracting its ideological "content," the larger purpose of his interest in the history of ideas may distort for some the poem's nature and make a small fish talk like a ponderous Johnsonian whale. Someone has observed that one of the limitations involved in studying the Elizabethan world picture is that one can then sometimes see nothing else, but G. A. Wilkes offers a useful corrective view. While conceding that *Orchestra* has a range of implications not nowadays associated with its subject, he adds:

. . . in Davies' adroit manipulation of these correspondences, we must not look for anything so solemn as a treatment of the theme of "order" under the symbol of the dance. The true motive of *Orchestra* . . . is one which governs more Elizabethan verse than we usually recognise. The fineness of the "invention" is what the Elizabethans would have prized: the cleverness of the analogies, the ingenuity of their elaboration, the brilliance with which the whole undertaking is sustained almost, in fact, "the daintiness of the device."[57]

For Wilkes, *Orchestra* is not a didactic work explicitly directed toward the exposition of the world order; rather, it is a poem in which ideas serve an "aesthetic" purpose, constituting the materials of a work "which has no end but its own excellence, and the pleasure its cleverness may give."[58] I am not sure that the late Professor Tillyard would have objected seriously to such a view. Enduring works of art speak on many levels and repay study from several points of view. But, in concluding our consideration of *Orchestra*, it is worth pursuing Wilkes' approach to the poem.

Most readers delight in Davies' high inventiveness as his imagination bodies forth the forms of things in ways scarcely thought of before, turning airy nothings into pleasing shapes. There is something of the magician's skill as he cleverly pulls one bright analogy after another out of an unpromising sleeve, as in these samples:

> Of all their ways, I love Meander's path,
> Which, to the tunes of dying swans doth dance
> Such winding sleights, such turns and tricks he hath,
> Such creeks, such wrenches, and such dalliance,
> That, whether it be hap or heedless chance,
> In his indented course and wriggling play
> He seems to dance a perfect cunning hay.   (St. 53)

✿   ✿   ✿

> What makes the vine about the elm to dance
> With turnings windings and embracements round?
> What makes the lodestone to the north advance
> His subtle point, as if from thence he found
> His chief attractive virtue to redound?
> Kind nature first doth cause all things to love;
> Love makes them dance, and in just order move.   (St. 56)

Davies' image-making ability is pleasantly demonstrated in these stanzas:

> For lo, the sea that fleets about the land
> And like a girdle clips her solid waist,
> Music and measure both doth understand;
> For his great crystal eye is always cast
> Up to the moon and on her fixed fast;
> And as she danceth in her pallid sphere,
> So danceth he about the centre here.[59]   (St. 49)

✿   ✿   ✿

> A diverse cause but like solemnity,
> Unto the temple leads the bashful bride,

Which blusheth like the Indian ivory
Which is with dip of Tyrian purple dyed;
A golden troop doth pass on every side
Of flourishing young men and virgins gay,
Which keep fair measure all the flow'ry way. (St. 90)

Several structural principles work not only to order the diverse
multiplicity of detail but also to set artful limits to Davies' play
of imagination. The central organizing idea is, of course, the
dance and the profusion of conceits Davies skillfully extracts
from it. But the poet artfully avoids monotony by distributing
the conceits according to another structural principle, that underlying the stages of Antinous' debate with Penelope, which ranges
from heaven to earth to man and from past to present, reconciling apparent "disorder and rout" with order and asserting the
creative and reconciling force of Love against a "mischievous
Lust." In addition, the debate is contained by the slight, and
incomplete, narrative structure which directs the whole poem
toward some final reply by Penelope to Antinous' invitation.

A variety of tonal effects develops as the poem unfolds. The
pervasive voice of the poet has two principal tones, one inspired
by Terpsichore, the poet's "light Muse" (St. 6); the other by
"Urania, prophetess divine" (St. 127). The first tone is a youthful, presumptuous, impudent one as Davies undertakes to correct
Homer's oversight; the other is a more serious ceremonial tone
that befits his celebration of the "heavenly state" of Elizabeth's
court which begins to form in the magic mirror. In addition,
within the bounds of Antinous' discourse, pleasing tonal variation occurs as his wooing modulates from polite address to
patient didacticism, to frustrated eagerness, to desperate petition.
The tonal variations constitute a significant source of the pleasure
we experience in reading the poem.

Perhaps the most delightful achievement of this graceful poem
is the imaginative "world," that totality of implication, which it
evokes. A world distinctly human, it is "tingling with anthro-
pomorphic life," as C. S. Lewis pleasingly described it,[60] in
which metaphor interanimates all being with human significance.
We easily accept the image of the sun as "a reveller in rich
array," dancing "his galliard" before his beloved Earth, and the

Sea with "his great crystal eye" gazing fixedly at the moon. "Some wits enrich'd with learning's skill" notwithstanding, the ancient Ptolemaic universe survives with earth and mankind comfortably at its center, and with all creation vibrant with meaning for human life. And it is a world made all the more convincing by the lucid, undistracting language which creates it, as Davies expresses his strange and sometimes extravagant wit in so probable a manner.

Death and the end of things are not totally excluded from this world of heart's desire, for at some "fatal instant" "all to nothing should again resolve" (St. 28), "The axletree of heaven shall break in twain" (St. 36), and "pale death" shall sever the "vital twist" of man's life (St. 60). But such events hover far in the distance, scarcely to be thought of—except to urge a keener delight in life and to teach a lady the wisdom of joining the dance of love.

CHAPTER 4

The Social Applications of Poetry

THE success a man like Davies sought in the courtly society
of Elizabethan England depended not only upon his means
and abilities but also upon his social connections. To stand out
in London among so many gifted and ambitious men demanded
the support and intercessory talents of a patron (or patrons),
one who had made his way up Fortune's hill and was willing to
give a hand up to another, perhaps by mentioning his name at
an opportune moment, by directing some preferment his way, by
introducing him to those who might also interest themselves in
his career—or, when one was in difficulty for having attacked
a fellow student at the Middle Temple—by exerting the right
pressure to restore one's lost opportunities.

We have already seen that Davies had succeeded in enlisting
the support of powerful and influential men, but of interest
is the part Davies' literary talents played in winning and main-
taining that support. The relationship of literature and patronage in this period is very important, and one which has received
considerable scholarly attention.[1] John F. Danby has formulated
an interesting classification of Elizabethan poets in terms of
their relationships to their society and to their patrons.[2] According to Danby, Sidney was a writer happily above the need for
patronage, for his favorable aristocratic position freed him from
having to cater to a particular audience. Consequently, his poetry
is devised chiefly to satisfy himself and his individual apprehension of truth. In contrast, Spenser's dedication to his poetic vision
of truth embraced a deeper concern about how that vision,
learnedly and artfully expressed, might impress Leicester or
Elizabeth with its author's mental abilities and flatter them with
so impressive a form of homage. Spenser's poetry bids for public
notice and national recognition: "Where Sidney was writing for

himself Spenser was writing for an audience; an audience, however, sage, sophisticated, serious, and civilized. He is the poet poeticizing in public."[3] Donne appears as a third type, a "gentleman-poet" who sought no particular reward or distinction for his poems as such, but employed his poetry "as a kind of leverage" to gain access to the houses of the great: "to grapple the rich prize to his heart with hoops of conceits."[4] In yet another category, Danby places poets like Ben Jonson and Shakespeare, professional writers whose careers patrons could enhance and make easier, but whose demonstrable talents and more or less steady employment in the theaters afforded them considerable independence in their work.

Davies best seems to take a position near Donne in Danby's third category, for much of his writing is directed toward the benefits that his witty and entertaining efforts might earn him from the great. His work was certainly not that of a man, sequestered from the concerns of getting on and pleasing others, who sought only the lonely personal satisfaction that verbal expression might afford. Rather, his poetry seems in large measure outwardly directed; it is prompted by a social muse to entertain his fellows with witty epigrams and parodies and to amuse a friend with an ingenious poem on dancing. Even so somber and philosophical a poem as *Nosce Teipsum* is clearly given a social context in its dedication to the Queen and in Davies' presenting manuscript gift copies to eminent men. But a number of his poems are even more overtly related to Davies' desire for promotion and for earning the good will of the powerful. These are works written as compliments or panegyrics, in honor of important occasions, and as social entertainments in the homes of important men.

I *The Poet as Celebrant*

One of the long-established modes of complimenting and flattering someone was through the formal dedication of a work to him. Presumably, the dedication was a gesture of the writer's esteem or his appreciation for a patron's encouragement and support. For one so honored the dedication was a source of social prestige for the recipient thought worthy of such a work. The

Gulling Sonnets, it will be recalled, bore a dedicatory sonnet to Sir Anthony Cooke, whose superior judgment, Davies indicated, would concur with his own contempt for "The bastard Sonnetts of these Rymers bace." As we have seen, *Orchestra* was first dedicated to Richard Martin, Davies' "very freind," whom the poet praised for his "mellifluous tongue." *Nosce Teipsum* was published with an elaborate thirty-four line dedication to Elizabeth. In it Davies offered his thoughts concerning the immortality of the soul:

> To the diuinest and the richest minde,
>   Both by Art's purchase and by Nature's dowre,
>   That euer was from Heau'n to Earth confin'd,
>   To shew the vtmost of a creature's power:

> To that great Spirit, which doth great kingdomes mooue,
>   The sacred spring whence right and honor streames,
>   Distilling Vertue, shedding Peace and Loue,
>   In euery place, as Cynthia sheds her beames.[5]

Climaxing his compliment, he wished the Queen,

> O! Many, many yeares may you remaine,
>   A happy angell to this happy Land;
>   Long, long may you on Earth our empresse raigne,
>   Ere you in Heauen a glorious angell stand.

> Stay long (sweet spirit) ere thou to Heauen depart,
>   Which mak'st each place a heauen wherein thou art.[6]

Thrifty in making one poem serve for more than one master, Davies had manuscript copies of *Nosce Teipsum* prepared for select individuals. One such copy is preserved at Holkham Hall (in Norfolk), and it has a dedication "To my honorable patron and frend Ed. Cooke, Esq., her M[ties] Attorney-Generall." A second copy can be found at Alnwick Castle dedicated "to the right noble, valorous, and learned Prince Henry, Earle of Northumberland."[7] Davies praised Northumberland for his "winged spirit" and for his desire "to learne and know the truth" of all things; moreover, it expressed his appreciation to one who "did protect me in distresse," presumably a reference to the troubled period following Davies' attack on Martin.[8] Two of Davies' later prose treatises bear significant dedications: *A Discoverie of the True Causes* was dedicated to King James, and *Le Primer Report des Cases* was prefaced by an "Epistle-Dedicatory" "To the Right Honovrable My Singvlar Good Lord, Thomas Lord Ellesmere, Lord Chancellor of England."

In addition, Davies wrote poems of overt praise and deliberate compliment; and Queen Elizabeth figures prominently as a subject for such efforts. Davies had earlier worked into   the texture of *Orchestra* graceful compliments to the Queen and her court, as Penelope beheld the image of "Our glorious English Courts diuine image, / As it should be in this our Golden Age" (St. 126), presided over by Elizabeth. Among his minor poems occur other tributes to the Queen. "To the Q[ueene]," for example, gracefully develops analogies between music and the Queen's harmonizing power over her kingdom:

> What Musicke shall we make to you?
> To whome the strings of all men's harts
> Make musicke of ten thousand parts:
> In tune and measure true,
> With straines and changes new.
>
> How shall wee fraime a harmony
> Worthie your eares, whose princely hands
> Keepe harmony in sundry lands:
> Whose people divers be,
> In station and degree?
> Heauen's tunes may onely please,
> and not such aires as theise.
>
> For you which downe from heauen are sent
> Such peace vpon the earth to bring,
> Haue h[e]ard ye quire of Angells sing:
> and all the sphaeres consent,
> Like a sweete instrument.
>
> How then should theise harsh tunes you heare
> Created of ye trubled ayer,
> breed but distand—when you repaire—

to your celestiall eare?
So that this center here
for you no musicke fynds,
but harmony of mynds.[9]

In addition, Elizabeth is probably the subject of "A Maid's Hymne in Praise of Virginity," as well as of "Elegies of Loue," both of which contain images of the sun's reviving the poet's Muse similar to those of the dedicatory verses of *Nosce Teipsum.*[10]

But it is in the *Hymnes of Astraea,*[11] published in 1599 some months following *Nosce Teipsum,* that Davies' most artfully sustained and concentrated adulation of the aging but still powerful Queen appears. The work is a series of twenty-six, sixteen-line poems each in three stanzas of five, five, and six lines. Davies set himself difficult limits within which to articulate his panegyrics. In all twenty-six Hymnes he follows a regular rhyme pattern of *AABAB CCDCD* in the first two stanzas, permitting occasional variations from the dominant pattern of *EEFGGF* in the third stanzas. The prevailing meter is iambic tetrameter, but considerable variation in meter occurs, perhaps because the poems were designed to be sung as "hymns." In addition, as an artfully clever compliment to Elizabeth, the poems are all acrostics: the initial letters of the lines read downward spell the royal name ELISABETHA REGINA, as in the following example:

Hymne II.

To Astraea.

Eternall Virgin, *Goddesse* true,
Let me presume to sing to you.
Ioue, euen great *Ioue* hath leasure
Sometimes to heare the vulgar crue,
And heares them oft with pleasure.

Blessèd *Astraea,* I in part
Enioy the blessings you impart;
The Peace, the milke and hony,
Humanitie, and civil *Art,*
A richer dower then money.

Right glad am I that now I liue,
Euen in these dayes whereto you giue
Great happinesse and glory;
If after you I should be borne,
No doubt I should my birth-day scorne,
Admiring your sweet storie.

Such verbal contrivance strikes some modern readers as an abuse of talent; as one critic puts it, they are "the last word in Elizabethan 'foppery,' "[12] or another, "a silly *tour de force* that vanishes from consciousness in proportion as it is successful."[13] But interest in such verbal tricks and complicated formal patterning was fashionable among the court poets of Davies' time. Like the mastery of prosody and the more traditional poetic forms, they were a part of the poet's competence in his craft, the manifestation of his "art" as a "maker."[14] While such cleverness was perhaps often more a matter of clever parlor entertainment than of serious concern, ingenious formal elements sometimes were involved with very great poems, such as the famous *Epithalamion* in which Spenser celebrates his own wedding day, and, as A. Kent Hieatt has so brilliantly demonstrated, correlates the poem's twenty-four stanzas with the twenty-four hours of his wedding day, even signaling the coming of night in the stanza appropriate to the exact hour in which night fell on his wedding day.[15]

Poetic tributes to Elizabeth came forth in profusion during her long reign.[16] Her significance for her subjects was complex. While many looked to her for special favors and, in serving and lauding her, no doubt sought chiefly their own advantage, many had a genuine admiration for her attractive personal qualities and talents, and respected her ability to bring England safely through perilous times. She was able to inspire tremendous efforts and daring in her courtiers and subjects, and the poets of the times wrote of her as if she were the object of some great chivalric love or religious adoration. Some addressed her as Cynthia, Diana, Phebe, Pandora, Gloriana; others deemed it appropriate to speak of her with the titles and expressions of worship usually reserved for the Virgin Mary. But Astraea, goddess of justice, and the rich associations that had grown up about her, attracted Davies as the most suitable analogy for his celebration of Elizabeth's regal qualities.[17]

In ancient Greek mythology, the virgin goddess Astraea—in some accounts, the daughter of Zeus and Themis; in others, of Astraeus the Titan and Eus, or Aurora—distributed blessings to mankind during the Golden Age. She withdrew to the mountains during the Silver Age; and, finally, offended by man's growing rapacities and violence, she fled to the heavens where she may be seen as the constellation Virgo. Various qualities attributed to her are reflected in such images as her crown of stars, recalling her "stellified" state; a pair of scales, representing her devotion to justice; and an ear of corn, suggesting the plenty of life's blessings which she had bestowed on man, especially during the halcyon days of the Golden Age.[18]

She figures in Virgil's influential Fourth Eclogue, which prophesies the advent of a new golden age of peace and political stability. In later writers, especially in Dante, Astraea is connected with imperial ideals of universal empire;[19] and, during the Renaissance, she is associated with Reformation ideas of the rebirth of a purified Christian faith and the synthesis of political and clerical rule.

In the *Hymnes,* Davies draws upon this rich complex of associations for the principal themes praising Elizabeth. We may discern a thematic ordering in the collection. The first two Hymnes establish the figure of Astraea as the controlling symbol for the work, a symbol to which Elizabeth is explicitly related by the acrostic on her name. Astraea is hailed as "The Mayd" who "Hath brought againe the golden dayes / And all the world amended" (Hymne I), who has imparted the blessings of "Peace, the milke and hony, / Humanitie, and civil *Art*" (Hymne II) to the land.

Hymnes III-XII are concerned primarily with Astraea/Elizabeth as she relates to or is reflected in the outer world. She is associated with such images of renewed life as the "Liuely Spring which makes all new" (Hymne III); the "sweet moneth of May" (Hymne IV); the morning Larke singing her praises to the heavens (Hymne V); the rose as the "Queen of flowres," the "Sweet nurse-child of the Spring's young howres" (Hymne VII); the flowering of the Muses, "The new fresh Howres and

Graces" at her court in Greenwich (Hymne IX); and the fruition and harvest time of September, the month of Elizabeth's birth (Hymne X).[20]

Hymne XII, which speaks of the inadequacy of a picture ("Rude counterfeit") justly to portray her true beauty, offers a transition to Hymnes XIII–XXV, which celebrate Elizabeth's unseen glories—her mental qualities (Hymnes XIII–XIX), the "passions of her Heart" "euer rul'd with Honor" (Hymne XX), and such regal qualities of character as wisdom, justice, magnanimity, and moderation (Hymnes XXI–XXV).

The series concludes, somewhat flatly, with a hymn addressed "To Enuy," in which the poet scorns invidious suggestions that his pen is for hire, and insists that he writes only from his genuine admiration. Although no evidence survives of Davies' reaping any special benefits from these "dainty trifles," we presume that the Queen was pleased to be honored in so ingenious a way. For most modern readers, the *Hymnes* probably are of interest chiefly as historical curiosities. But occasionally we come across one or two of the *Hymnes*, such as III and V, which retain intrinsic poetic charm.

II A Poet for All Occasions

Davies wrote some poems which might best be called "occasional," that is, poems written for particular events. It is likely that Davies wrote more of this kind of poetry than has survived. Although much of what is extant is not very impressive, it does offer another indication of the social applications Davies made of his poetic talents.

For the publication of *Ovid's Banquet of Sense* (1595) by fellow poet George Chapman, Davies contributed two prefatory sonnets of commendation.[21] He sent a sonnet of condolence to Ellesmere, his loyal supporter, entitled "On the Death of Lord Chancellor Ellesmere's Second Wife in 1599." Signed "Yr. Lps in all humble Duties and condoling with yr. Lp. most affectionately Jo. Davys," the poem says more of the living than of the dead; it focuses more on the Chancellor's qualities of mind and heart than on the loss of his wife:

> You that in Judgement passion neuer show,
> (As still a Judge should without passion bee),
> So judge your self; and make not in your woe
> Against your self a passionate decree.
> Griefe may become so weake a spirit as mine:
> My prop is fallne, and quenched is my light:
> But th' Elme may stand, when with'red is the vine,
> And, though the Moone eclipse, the Sunne is bright.
> Yet were I senseless if I wisht your mind,
> Insensible, that nothing might it moue;
> As if a man might not bee wise and kind.
> Doubtlesse the God of Wisdome and of Loue,
> As Solomon's braine he doth to you impart,
> So hath he given you David's tender hart.[22]

John Payne Collier reprinted from Ellesmere's papers the following interesting note which was appended to the sonnet: "A French Writer (whom I love well) speakes of three kindes of Companions, Men Women, and Bookes: the losse of this second makes you retire from the first: I haue, therefore presum'd to send y[r] Lp one of the third kind w[ch] (it may bee), is a stranger to your Lp. yet I persuade me his conversation will not be disagreeable to y[r] Lp."[23]

In addition to Davies' journeying with others to Scotland to meet with James after the Queen's death, Davies greeted James and his queen on their "first coming into England" with two poems. Both written in the stanza form of *Nosce Teipsum*, they are entitled "The Kinges Welcome" and "To the Queene at the Same Time."[24] In the first, Davies sends his "gentle muse" to find the king, who will be readily recognized by "his reall markes and true":

> Looke ouer all that divers troope, and finde
> whoe hath his spirites most Jouiall and free,
> whose bodie is best tempred, and whose minde
> Is ever best in tune, and that is hee.
>
> See who it is whose actions doe bewraye
> that threefold power, which rarely mixt we see;
> a iudgment graue, and yet a fancie gaye,
> Joynd with a ritch remembrance, that is hee.

Marke who it is, that hath all noble skill,
which maye to publique good referrèd bee;
the quickest witt, and best affected will,
whence flowes a streame of vertues, that is hee.

If any more then other clearely wise
or wisely iust or iustly valiant be;
If any doe fainte pleasures more despise,
or be more maister of himselfe, 'tis hee.[25]

Davies extolls the king for nine more stanzas; and, although such open courting of a superior's favor may seem excessive and repulsive today, it was commonplace in Jacobean times; and Davies' poem is no more fulsome than many similar expressions from the aspiring.[26]

Other of his occasional poems concern royal tributes. On James' death, Davies not only hastened to kiss the hand of his new king, Charles I, but also wrote poems for him, such as *"Mira Loquor Sol Occubuit Nox Nulla Secuta Est,"* "Charles His Waine," and "Of the Name of Charolus, Being the Diminative of Charus."[27] Perhaps the light and witty "Verses Sent to the Kinge With Figges: By S[r] John Davis" was also directed to Charles. Although Grosart offers no comment about them, "The Faire Ladyes," "Upon a Paire of Garters," and "To His Lady-Love" are apparently "occasional" verse.[28]

Davies' most significant and interesting occasional poem, published for the first time only a few years ago, is an epithalamion written to celebrate an important wedding among the nobility. This poem is found in Leweston Fitzjames' commonplace book, which, as noted earlier, preserves the texts of the *Epigrams* and *Orchestra*. Falconer Madan mentioned the poem in his catalogue description of the manuscript,[29] but it received no careful attention or discussion until the Reverend Childs' study of Davies.[30] In 1962, Robert Krueger published a transcription of the text.[31]

The poem is headed: *"Epithalamion Io: Dauisij,"* and its conclusion is marked *"Finis 95. Ian:."* Fitzjames was Davies' fellow student at the Middle Temple and would probably have known Davies' poetry well. His attribution, accepted both by Childs and by Krueger, seems reliable. In addition, as Krueger points out,[32] the "Epithalamion" contains diction, ideas, and images quite similar to those in *Orchestra*, similarities that suggest a common authorship for the two poems and a date of composition for the "Epithalamion" near that of *Orchestra*.

The "Epithalamion" has genuine charm and merit. Since it is relatively unfamiliar and less readily accessible than Davies' other poems, I reproduce the text below transcribed from Fitzjames' commonplace book (fols. 49ʳ–51ʳ):[33]

Epithalamion Io:Dauisij

Loue not that Loue that is a child and blynde,
But that Heroicke honorable Loue,
Which first the fightinge Elements combinde,
And taught the world in harmony to moue
    That God of Loue whose sweet attractiue power
    First founded cityes, and societyes,
    Which linkes trewe frendes, and to each paramor,
    (That virtewe loues)a virtewous Loue affies.
This Loue hath causd the Muses to record,
Their sweetest tuens and most celestiall,   [10]
To you sweet Lady, and to you great Lorde,
In honor of your joyfull nuptiall.
    And to their tuens this prayer they still apply,
    That with your dayes your joyes maye multiplye.

Clio.

Illustrious Lord heire of that happy race,
Which with great Lordshipps doth great Loue inherit,
Raysd by the heavens vnto that glorious place,
Which your great grawnseirs did by virtewe merit.
    And you sweete Lady virtewes noble fayre,
    Whome when I name, your grandsier, father, Mother,   [20]
    (Of all whose excellencies you are heire,)
    I then extoll, and prayse aboue all other,
Your famous Auncestors eternall names,
My diamond pen in adamant shall write,
And I will spread your owne younge louing fames,
As far as *Phœbus* spreades his glorious light
    Still with my tuens importuninge the skye,
    That with your dayes your Joyes maye multiplye.

Thalia.

And I the merry Muse of Comedyes,
That with a marriage euer end my playe,   [30]
Will into mirth and greatest joye arise,
While I applawd this blessed marriage daye,
   Yet will I sadly praye my Father Joue,
   That as crosse chaunce fought not agaynst your will,
   In the fayre course of your most happy Loue,
   So with out crosse ye maye continewe still.
That as the voyce and *Echo* doe agree,
So maye you both, both doe, and saye the same,
And as your eyes beinge two, but one thinge see,
So maye ye to one end your actions frame,
   So shall your lyves be a sweete harmonye,   [40]
   And with your dayes your Joyes shall multiplye.

Melpomene.

And I which sownd the tragicke tuens of ware,
Haue layd my harsh and fearfull Trumpe aside,
Wher with I vsd to rende the ayre a fare,
In seruice of your cosin bewtious bride.
   Your most victorious cosin warlike Vere,
   The glory of your glorious familye,
   A brauer spirit the earth did neuer beare,
   Since first the fyer of lyfe came from the skye,   [50]
This fyery starre of *Mars* my trumpett tooke,
And put a warblinge lute betwine my handes,
And with a joyfull voyce and joyfull looke,
Sent me to blesse these sacred marriage bandes,
   And to commend his vowes to Joue on hie,
   That with your dayes your joyes maye multiplye.

Euterpe.

And I betwine whose lipps the ayre doth playe,
Chaunginge her wanton forme ten thousand wayes,
Will not distingwish one halfe note this daye,
Which shall not sownd both to your joye and prayse,   [60]
   For euen your marriage doth sweete musicke make,
   Like two sweete notes matcht in an vnisone,
   Where each from other doth full sweetnesse take,
   Where one could make no harmony aloane,

Longe maye you Joye such sympathye of Loues,
As doth betwine the Elme and Vine remayne,
Or betwine palme trees, twinns, and turtle doues,
Wher in one lyfe doth live the lives of twayne,
   Longe live you in each other mutually,
   That with your dayes your Joyes maye multiplye.   [70]

Terpsichore.

And I whose cunninge feete with measurd motion,
Expresse the musicke which my Sisters singe
Will nowe in songes expresse my trewe devotion,
To you which to my Arte most honor bringe,
   For who can dawnce with better skill and [grace],
   Then you great bridgroome or then you fayr bride,
   Whether a solleme measure ye doe pase,
   Or els with swifter tuens more swiftly slide.
Still maye you dawnce and keepe that measure still,
In all your lyfe which you in dawncinge shewe,   [80]
Where both the man and woman haue one will,
And both at once the selfe same paces goe.
   So shall you never drawe your yoke awry,
   But with your dayes, your joyes shall multiply.

Erato.

And I the waytinge mayde of bewtyes Queene,
Which oft am wonte to singe of wanton Loue,
Since I these sacred nuptials haue seene,
An other godhead in my brest doth moue,
   For nowe I singe of bewty of the minde,
   Which bewtifies the fayrest outward bewty,   [90]
   And of a passion which is neuer blinde
   But waytes on virtewe with respectfull dutye.
O sacred Love wher one loves only one,
Where each to other is a mirror fayre,
Wherin them selues are each to other shone,
Such is your sacred loue illustrious payre,
   Whose fyer like *Vestas* flame shall neuer dye,
   But with your dayes your joyes shall multiplye.

Polyhimnia.

And I which with my gesture seeme to speake,
Will speake indeede in honor of this daye,   [100]

Which shall to *Ioue* passe through the milkey waye.
 Euen to the eares of *Ioue* my tuens shall come
 And be for you (sweet bride) a zealous praier
 That as a cherye graft vppon a plumme,
 You maye be fruitfull in your issues fayre.
Or that you and your Love be like two streames,
Which meeting after many windes and crookes,
Doe spread their mingled waues through many realmes,
And from them selues diriue a thousande brookes,   [110]
 And though the lesser loose her name therby,
 Yet with her dayes, her Joyes shall multiplye.

Calliope.

And I which singe th' eroicke Loue of Kinges,
Must vse like notes whiles I your names rehearse,
For he which your great names in number singes,
With names of Princes doth adorne his verse.
 And princly is your match as gold and Pearle,
 Both bewtifull each other bewtifie,
 So an earls daughter married to an Erle,
 Giues and receaues like honor mutually.   [120]
And as the purest cullors which alone,
Sett by themselves imperfect bewty make,
Wher they are mingled and conjoynd in one,
One from an other lyfe and lustre take,
 So you beinge matcht each other glorifie,
 That with your dayes your Joyes maye multiplye.
And with my sweetest tuens the ayre will breake,

Vrania.

But I the Muse of Heauen to heauen will rayse [you]
And your fayre names in starry letters write,
That they which dwell vnder both poles maye prayse you,
And in rehearsall of your names delight.   [130]
 And you fayre Bride shall like fayre *Cynthia* sh[ine]
 Which beinge in conjunction with the Sunne,
 Doth seeme her beames & glory to resigne,
 But hath indeede more light and virtewe wonne.
Longe shall you shine on earth like Lampes of heaven,
Which when you leaue, I will you stellifie,
To you sweete bride shall *Hebes* place be giuen,
But your Lord shall his *Ganimedes* roome supplye.

Till when I will invoke each dyetye,
That with your Dayes your joyes maye multipl(ye)   [140]

Finis. 95. Ian:

The likely occasion for this poem can be determined by two significant allusions in the fourth and ninth sonnets, and the event is confirmed by Fitzjames' date. Melpomene states that she has put aside her "harsh and fearfull Trumpe," which she had used in the service of the bride's "most victorious cosin warlike Vere," an allusion to Francis Vere (1560–1609), the "illustrious Vere" mentioned in Davies' "Epigram No. 40."[34] Calliope, accustomed to "singe th'eroicke Loue of Kinges," offers to "vse like notes" for this couple because "an earls daughter married to an Erle, / Gives and receaves like honor mutually." These allusions and the date of 1595 point to the wedding of Elizabeth Vere, daughter of the seventeenth Earl of Oxford and the granddaughter of William Cecil, Lord Burghley, to William Stanley, sixth Earl of Derby. The wedding took place at Greenwich on January 26, 1595.[35] Its prominence and the prestige of the families involved interestingly reflect the important social and political circles whose attention Davies was attracting by his verse.

Davies' "Epithalamion" is of considerable historical interest as an early example in English of a kind of poem soon to become quite popular. Students of this ancient form have traced its origin back to early nuptial folk songs. As its literal meaning suggests, it was a special marriage song sung "at the bridal chamber," prior to the consummation of the marriage, and perhaps as an evocation of fertility. By the time Sappho was writing epithalamia—only fragments of which have survived—the term had broadened to include several kinds of songs customary at weddings. Early in its history, the epithalamion treated fictive as well as real weddings, as in Theocritus' Eighteenth Eclogue, which concerns the wedding of Helen and Menelaus. It was also incorporated into dramas and narrative poems. Among Latin poets, Ovid, Statius, and Claudius further developed the form, but it was Catullus' nuptial poems *Carmina* 61, 62, and 64 which exerted the greatest influence on Renaissance

writers of epithalamia. In the fifteenth century, Continental
neo-Latin poets imitated these poems of Catullus; and, in the
following century, Tasso in Italy and the Pléiade poets in France
wrote such poems in their vernaculars. The epithalamion had,
thus, become a recognized kind of poem, one of importance
because of its Classical precedents, recent examples by major
poets, and critical attention by Scaliger in *Poeticus libri septem*
(1561).

The form was not naturalized in English until Sir Philip
Sidney wrote the first formal English epithalamion, the pastoral
song among the Third Eclogues of *Arcadia* (1593) that is sung
by Dicus for the marriage of Kala and Lalus. Spenser's much
greater *Epithalamion,* published with his *Amoretti* in 1595,
is the only other known example prior to Davies' poem. Thereafter the epithalamion enjoyed a considerable vogue; and most
of the major and many of the minor poets of the sixteenth and
seventeenth centuries wrote such nuptial poems.[36]

As a student of contemporary English poetry, Davies may
well have known Spenser's poem and been influenced in a general
way by it. Spenser's great achievement may have illustrated
the epithalamion's potentials and thereby encouraged Davies
to attempt one. In certain technical matters, such as the complex
stanzas interlinked by a common refrain, Davies may have
found some suggestions for his own poem. Aside from these rather
general possibilities, however, I find no evidence of Davies'
specific indebtedness to Spenser's poem; but there seems more
reason to think that Davies did owe some debt to Sidney's
"Songe" assigned to Dicus in the *Arcadia.* In *Orchestra,* under
the name of Astrophel, Davies had praised Sidney, "Whose supple
Muse Camelion-like doth change / Into all formes of excellent
deuise"; and it is likely that he knew the poems Sidney had
included in his complex pastoral romance *Arcadia.*

Dicus's "Songe" is a series of eleven nine-line stanzas, rhyming
ABABBCCDD, each concluding with the line: "O *Himen* long
their coupled joyes maintaine," a refrain similar to Davies'.[37]
While there are many important differences, there are also
some interesting parallels in idea and image between the two
poems. In the opening sonnet, Davies distinguishes between
"that Love that is a child and blynde" and "that Heroicke

honorable Love" which brought order and harmony to the "fighting Elements." Sidney opens his poem by distinguishing between "justest love" and "Cupid's powers," the former having "vanquished" the latter, whose "warr of thoughts is swallow'd up in peace" (ll. 4–5). Of love's union, Davies' Euterpe sings: "Longe maye you Joye such sympathye of Loues, / As doth betwine the Elm and Vine remayne" (ll. 65–66): Dicus wishes that Kala and Lalus "may ever bide, like to the Elme and vyne, / With mutuall embracements them to twyne" (ll. 14–16). The merging of rivers figures in both poems, the image serving as a vehicle for different tenors: Polyhimnia pictures the fruitful issue of the marriage, wishing

> . . . that you and your Love be like two streames,
> Which meeting after many windes and crookes,
> Doe spread their mingled waves through many realmes,
> And from themselves dirive a thousand brookes. . . .   (ll. 106–9)

Dicus uses the analogy as an illustration of the lovers' union in death:

> Let one time (but long first) close up their daies,
>   One grave their bodies seaze:
>   And like two rivers sweete,
>   When they though divers do together meete:
>   One streame both streames containe,
>   O *Himen* long their coupled joyes maintaine.   (ll. 31–35)

While such images can be found elsewhere and are perhaps among a common store drawn upon by many poets of the time, it may be that they are echoes of Sidney in "Epithalamion," as Davies attempted, for himself and English poetry, a new kind of poem.

Davies' idea of developing his poem as a series of songs sung by the Muses probably owes something to other writers and to general tradition. Spenser had recently summoned the same goddesses in *The Teares of the Muses* (1591), albeit for a series of lugubrious laments about the contemporary disregard of poetry. In a note to Spenser's poem in the Variorum Edition, W. L. Renwick suggests a possible indebtedness by Spenser to

Ronsard's *Dialogue entre les Muses Deslogées et Ronsard;* but
he observes that the idea is not a recondite one and that
George Buchanan and others had also employed these goddesses
for courtly pageantry.[38] In a study of Renaissance epithalamia,
Virginia Tufte finds among French wedding poems a fairly
frequent use of alternating choruses sung by river nymphs,
shepherds, virgins, and the Muses. Particularly interesting is
Antoine de Baïf's "Epithalame. À Monsieur Morel Ambrunoys,"
which opens with a stanza by Apollo, followed by one from
each of the nine Muses, and closes with one by Himen.[39]
Whatever anticipations there may have been of his idea, Davies
employs it skillfully to pay a graceful and dignified compliment
to his social betters, Elizabeth, William, and their distinguished
families.

In the course of the poem, Davies develops many of the
themes which had become conventional to the formal epithalamion; but, by assigning them to the individual goddesses, he adds
a quasi-dramatic effect to the lyric character of the individual
songs. Davies observes a degree of dramatic decorum by accom-
modating the song to the singer, assigning them "tuens" relevant
to their traditional interests in the arts. Clio, as the Muse of
History, appropriately recalls and lauds the couple's "famous
Auncestors eternall names"; and Urania, the "Muse of Heaven,"
offers to "stellifie" the couple at their deaths and to write their
"fayre names in starry letters." In fact, we can easily imagine
Davies' "Epithalamion" *performed* as a pageant-like entertainment in which young ladies appropriately costumed and bearing
identifying emblems—Melpomene's lute, Euterpe's flute, and
so forth—actually sang their songs before the bridal couple
and their guests.[40]

Varied by the idea and speakers, the poem is unified in
several ways. First, a dignified, formal, "proper" tone prevails
throughout as appropriate to the celebration of such an important
social occasion by a young man of Davies' social position. The
poet, who avoids any detailed consideration of the physical
aspects of the marriage, omits the anatomical inventory of the
bride or suggestive playfulness concerning the consummation
of the marriage, motifs which occur fairly frequently in other
epithalamia. Erato is properly on her good behavior: instead

"of wanton love," she sings of "bewty of the minde." And Thalia, the Muse of Comedy, is modest and dignified in her mirth.

Not only the tone but also several formal elements serve to unify the poem. There is, for example, a discernible order in the series of songs. Following the introductory sonnet, the songs move in temporal order from past, to present, to future; that is, from praise of the couple's ancestry and the occasion of the marriage, to comments concerning the marriage relationship, to a wish that the union be fruitful and that its issue bring honor to the couple, to a conclusion promising the couple's elevation to heaven following a hope for long life on earth. Moreover, as in other of his works, Davies set rigid and difficult formal limits within which to develop his poem. Each of the songs is a "Shakespearean" sonnet—another reminder of Davies' facility in adapting the sonnet to a variety of purposes. All of the sonnets have identical rhyme patterns and are gracefully linked by the recurring refrain.

The images which develop the theme of love's union and order, as well as the praise sung throughout, give unity to the poem. Following the initial statement praising love as the force which "first the fighting Elements combined, / And taught the world in harmony to move," Thalia wishes that the couple's love will continue without "crosse chaunce," and

> That as the voyce and *Echo* doe agree,
> So maye you both, both doe, and saye the same,
> And as your eyes beinge two, but one thinge see,
> So maye ye to one end your actions frame,
>   So shall your lyves be a sweet harmonye....

Euterpe develops the analogy between the union of music and that of marriage:

> For euen your marriage doth sweete musicke make,
> Like two sweete notes matcht in an vnisone,
> Where each from other doth full sweetnesse take,
> Where one could make no harmony aloane....

Terpsichore, predictably, pictures love's union in terms of the ordered movements of the dance:

> Still maye you dawnce and keepe that measure still,
> In all your lyfe which you in dawncinge shewe,
> Where both the man and woman haue one will,
> And both at once the selfe same paces goe.

Erato praises their "sacred Love," "Where each to other is a mirror fayre, / Wherin them selves are each to other shone." Polyhimnia's wish, as already noted, pictures the lovers and their fruitful issue as two rivers becoming one. Finally, Calliope sings that the lovers' relationship will give beauty to each party, as

> . . . the purest cullors which alone,
> Sett by themselves imperfect bewty make,
> Wher they are mingled and conjoynd in one,
> One from an other lyfe and lustre take. . . .

Davies' "Epithalamion" is a graceful achievement and additional evidence of the range of his poetic competence.

III   *Poet as Entertainer*

In the second edition of *A Poetical Rhapsody* (1608), Francis Davison added three interesting minor works by Davies: *Yet Other Twelve Wonders of the World*, *A Lotterie*, and *A Contention betwixe a Wife, a Widdowe and a Maide*.[41] These are "occasional" pieces, but of a special sort: they were devised as entertainments or amusements for guests at the houses of eminent political figures. As such, they are also indications of the access to important people that Davies' poetic talents gave the aspiring lawyer.

Yet Other Twelve Wonders of the World consists of twelve, six-line verse "characters," brief portraits of the Courtier, Divine, Soldier, Lawyer, Physician, Merchant, Country Gentleman, Bachelor, Married Man, Wife, Widow, and Maid. Each of the "Wonders" speaks for himself and is a "wonder" because he so ideally represents his type. Since there is a mild flicker of social satire about these sketches, they might be regarded as inverted satirical epigrams. Instead of detailing the departures of a Rufus or a Ponticus from a standard of good taste or prudence, Davies has each speaker define that standard indirectly by listing the modes of conduct each avoids—a technique that recalls Chaucer's in his descriptions of such pilgrims as the Clerk and Parson in the *General Prologue*. The two following sketches illustrate Davies' approach:

III. *The Souldier.*

My occupation is, the noble trade of Kings,
The tryall that decides the highest right of things:
Though *Mars* my master be, I doe not *Venus* loue,
Nor honor *Bacchus* oft, nor often sweare by *Ioue*;
Of speaking of my selfe, I all occasion shunne,
And rather loue to doe, then boast what I haue done.

IV. *The Lawyer*

The Law my calling is, my robe, my tongue, my pen,
Wealth and opinion gaine, and make me Iudge of men.
The knowne dishonest cause, I neuer did defend,
Nor spun out sutes in length, but wisht and sought an end:
Nor counsell did bewray, nor of both parties take,
Nor euer tooke I fee for which I neuer spake.[42]

Some useful evidence about the occasional nature of these sketches is found in an early seventeenth-century manuscript at Downing College, Cambridge. The manuscript is headed "Verses giuen to the L. Treasurer vpon a dosen of Trenchers by Mr. Davis."[43] Although the manuscript does not indicate which New Year's Day was so observed, Grosart proposes 1600 on the basis of the following letter in Davies' hand that was written to Sir Michael Hicks, secretary to Thomas Sackville, Lord Buckhurst, the Lord Treasurer:

Mr. Hicks. I have sent you heer inclosed that cobweb of my invention which I promised before Christmas: I pray you present it, commend it, and grace it, as well for your owne sake as mine: bycause by your nominacion I was first put to this taske, for which I acknowledge my self beholding to you in good earnest, though the imployment be light and trifling, because I am glad of any occasion of being made knowne to that noble gentl. whom I honore and admire exceedingly. If ought be to be added, or alter'd lett me heare

from you. I shall willingly attend to doo it, the more speedily if it
be before the terme. So in haste I comment my best service to you.
Chancery Lane, 20 Jan. 1600. Yours to do you service very willingly,
Jo. Davys.[44]

Grosart suggests that the "cobweb" of Davies' "invention" is
the *Twelve Wonders,* a view shared by other scholars.[45] Interestingly enough, such a set of trenchers, believed to have belonged
to Sackville, has survived and may be seen in Room 54 among
the Tudor and Early Stuart collection at the Victoria and Albert
Museum, London.[46] The trenchers and their container are in
ebony beechwood and are ornamented in gold. Each of the
trenchers bears a representation of the Wonder and the appropriate verses. The following note accompanies the Museum
exhibit:

Elizabethan dinner-parties, especially at the New Year, were often
followed by a "banquet" of Marchpane and other sweetmeats, somewhat similar to dessert. The Trenchers were decorated "on their
back sides" with designs and inscriptions intended to raise a laugh
as each guest turned up his own "lot." They were often made for
amusement or suited to facetious subjects modelled in confectionery
(*e.g.,* the Signs of the Zodiac). The trade of trencher-makers pre-
ferred old-fashioned themes, especially Bible texts, Aesop's fables,
the "language of flowers," proverbs, and the like. Family "lots" were
sometimes kept for generations.
A fashion for "characters" followed Casaubon's *Theophrastus*
(1592) and other works. The verses in this beechwood set were
written especially for trenchers at a New Year Party, probably in
1600, by Thomas Sackville, first Earl of Dorset, who had succeeded
Burghley as Lord Treasurer the previous year.

In addition to such visual treatment, the *Twelve Wonders* were
set to music by the lutenist John Maynard as *The XII Wonders
of the World. For the Violl de Gamba, the Lute, and the Voyce*
(1611).[47]
Queen Elizabeth was a mobile monarch. During her long
reign, she frequently moved her Court from Whitehall to
Greenwich, Richmond, Hampton Court, or Windsor; and she
visited other royal houses or private homes near London. The

moves afforded her a change of scene and a useful visibility among her subjects, who flocked to see, to speak to, and even to touch their revered ruler as she traveled from one residence to another. During the summer months, more extended travel was possible; and the queen with her extensive retinue went on "progresses" about the countryside, visiting the universities, enjoying the well-meant but sometimes clumsy hospitality of towns and local gentry, as well as the elaborate and, indeed, lavish receptions afforded her by national political figures at their rural estates.[48]

Such visits conferred honor on the hosts and, not infrequently, exacted heavy expenditures as they sought to entertain the Queen in suitable style. While Leicester's incredible extravagance during the Queen's three-week visit to Kennilworth in 1575 was not to be equaled, others who had enjoyed Elizabeth's favored attention—or wanted to enjoy it—were willing to spend considerable sums to make her visits memorable. According to J. E. Neale, Sir Nicholas Bacon, for an example, spent £577 for the Queen's four-days' visit in 1577; Burghley over £1000 for her ten-day visit in 1591; and Sir Thomas Egerton £2000 for her three-day visit in 1602.[49]

In addition to feeding and housing the large Royal party accompanying the Queen, the hosts were expected to bestow gifts and to amuse her with carefully planned entertainments. Among the gifts Sir Thomas Egerton gave Elizabeth during a visit in 1595 were a fine fan with a handle set with diamonds, a jewel with diamond pendants valued at £400, a pair of virginals, and an expensive gown.[50] The entertainments, sometimes very elaborate, featured poems and orations of greeting and farewell, singing, instrumental music, dancing, masques, plays, pageants, and spectacles occasionally requiring the participation of hundreds.

From July 31 to August 3, 1602, the Queen visited Harefield House, Egerton's estate in Middlesex.[51] The Lord Keeper seems to have turned to his witty protegé John Davies for assistance in entertaining his important guest. The poet's response, assuming the "I.D." signed to the work in Davison's *A Poetical Rhapsody*[52] refers to Davies, was *A Lotterie*.[53] Davies' *Lotterie* opens with "A Marriner" approaching the Queen, her maids of

honor, and other ladies bearing a box of gifts and "lots," or
chances, "supposed to come from the Carrick," an allusion to
a Spanish plate ship which the English had captured in June,
1602,[54] much to the delight and profit of the Queen. Before
offering the lots to the ladies, the Mariner sings the following
song, predictably complimentary to Elizabeth:

> *Cynthia* Queene of Seas and Lands,
> That fortune euery where commands,
> Sent forth fortune to the Sea,
> To try her fortune euery way.
> There did I fortune meet, which makes me now to sing,
> There is no fishing to the Sea, nor seruice to the King.
>
> All the Nymphs of *Thetis* traine
> Did *Cinthias* fortunes entertaine:
> Many a Iewell, many a Iem,
> Was to her fortune brought by them.
> Her fortune sped so well, as makes me now to sing,
> There is no fishing to the Sea, nor seruice to the King.
>
> Fortune that it might be seene,
> That she did serue a royall Queene,
> A franke and royall hand did beare,
> And cast her fauors euery where.
> Some toyes fell to my share, which makes me now to sing,
> There is no fishing to the Sea nor seruice to the King.[55]

The Mariner explains that the gifts had come into his hands
by Fortune and that he had vowed not to part with them "but
by Fortune." Finding himself by chance to have "lighted into
the best company of the world, a company of the fairest
Ladyes that euer I saw," he decides to offer the lots to them.
Twenty-nine of the thirty-four lots name gifts—"A Purse" (no. 2),
"A Looking-Glasse" (no. 4), "A Snuftkin" (no. 22); the remaining five are blanks, perhaps affording some sense of chance to the
drawing.[56] Each of the lots is accompanied by a pair of iambic
pentameter couplets, miniature verse mottoes or poesies, which
wittily—or nearly so—play on the gift named, usually offer a
compliment to the drawer, and relate the lot to the theme of
Fortune. The following are fair samples:

4. *A Looking-Glasse.*

Blinde Fortune doth not see how faire you be,
But giues a glasse that you your self may see.

❉ ❉ ❉

11. *A Paire of Kniues.*

Fortune doth giue this paire of Kniues to you,
To cut the thred of loue, if't be not true.

❉ ❉ ❉

20. *A Chaine.*

Because you scorne loue's Captiue to remaine,
Fortune hath sworne to leade you in a Chaine.

Hardly an important achievement, *A Lotterie* is a clever, if ephemeral, bit of piece-work done to order to provide a momentary amusement similar, perhaps, to that afforded today by the gnomic pronouncements found in Chinese fortune cookies. Elizabeth and her companions probably enjoyed the flattery and the wholesomely decorous wit treating the reportedly conventional interests of women.

The *Lotterie* seems, however, to have been only a part of the entertainment which Egerton provided the Queen during this visit. John Nichols printed from an early seventeenth-century manuscript found at the house of Sir Roger Newdigate, a later resident at Harefield House, an account headed *"Entertainment of Q. Eliz. at Harefield, by the Countesse of Derby."*[57] Grosart subsequently reprinted this item from Nichols and attributed it and the *Lotterie* to Davies.[58] The Newdigate manuscript, which makes no mention of *A Lotterie,* includes two prose dialogues, two songs, and one prose speech. On the Queen's arrival, and while she was still on horseback, a Bailiff and a Dairymaid, engaging in a rustic discussion of some strangers who had just arrived, describe the Queen as "the best Huswife in all this company." After the Queen had alighted from her horse and approached the house, where a carpet and chair had been placed for her, "Place," *"in a partie-colored roabe, like the brick house,"* and "Time," *"with yeollow haire, and in a*

green roabe, with a hower glasse, stopped, not runninge,"
engage in a second dialogue praising the "Goddesse" who had
so enriched the time and place by her visit. Both dialogues
conclude with presentations of jewelry to Elizabeth.

Following the dialogues in the manuscript is *"The humble
Petition of a guiltless Lady, delivered in writing vpon Munday
Morninge, when the robe of rainbowes was presented to the Q.
by the La. Walsingham.* The "Petition" consists of six, six-line
stanzas, opening with the following address to the sixty-nine-
year-old monarch:

> Beauties rose, and vertues booke,
> Angells minde, and Angells looke,
>   To all Saints and Angells deare,
> Clearest Maiestie on earth,
> Heauen did smile at your faire birth,
>   And since, your daies have been most cleare.

The "Petition" takes note of the rainy weather; relates the
colorful presentation robe to the rainbow; and, painfully, puns
on "rain" and Elizabeth's "reign."

At her departure, Elizabeth is confronted once again by Place,
"attyred in black mourninge aparell," who bids her farewell,
and presents her with a jewelled anchor. Concluding the
Entertainment is a song, "The Complaint of the Satyres Against
the Nymphs," which opens "Tell me, O Nymphes, why do you/
Shune vs that your loues pursue?" Grosart suggests that this song
was probably part of a Masque presented during the visit;[59]
but it should be noted that the song appears on a separate leaf
in the manuscript and is written in a different hand, thereby
suggesting that it may not actually have been a part of the
Harefield Entertainment.[60]

Grosart concedes that the omission of *A Lotterie* from the
"Entertainment" suggests that Davies was the author only
of the former. But he contends that *A Lotterie* probably served
as an amusement on one of the rainy days—noted in the
"Petition"—and that "the speeches and other things of the 'Entertainment' took place without doors, and distinct from the
Lottery."[61] The bases for his attribution of the entire Entertain-

ment to Davies are stylistic ones: "there are manifold marks that the whole came from one pen, and that pen Davies's; for throughout there is likeness of style and thought to his avowed writings."[62] Grosart cites a number of parallel passages, which, however, did not prove to be sufficiently cogent to convince Sir E. K. Chambers.[63] Certainty about such matters of attribution is difficult, if not impossible, to reach. Grosart's parallel passages point to Davies as the likely author. While there is no reason to think Davies could not or did not write the whole entertainment, thinking he did so adds little to his stature as a writer.

On December 6, 1602, Elizabeth dined with Sir Robert Cecil at Cecil House, the Secretary of State's handsome new residence in the Strand. As a part of the housewarming festivities, Cecil had "great varietie of entertainment prepared for her and many rich jewells and presents."[64] Concerning this event the lawyer John Manningham wrote in his diary:

> On Munday last the Queene dyned at Sir Robert Secils [*sic*] newe house in the Stran. Shee was verry royally entertained, richely presented, and marvelous well contented, but at hir departure shee strayned hir foote. His hall was well furnished with choise weapons, which hir Majestie tooke speciall notice of. Sundry deuises; at hir entraunce, three women, a maid, a widdowe, and a wife, eache commending their owne states, but the Virgin preferred; an other, on attired in habit of a Turke desyrous to see hir Majestie, but as a straunger without hope of grace, in regard of the retired manner of hir Lord, complained; answere made, howe gracious hir Majestie in admitting to presence, and howe able to discourse in anie language; which the Turke admired, and, admitted, presents hir with a riche mantle, &c.[65]

The device of the three women "commending their owne states" was one of Davies' contributions to the festivities known as *A Contention betwixt a Wife, a Widdowe and a Maide*, which John Chamberlain described as "a pretty dialogue."[66] Consisting of sixty quatrains, the *Contention* opens on "Astreas holy day" as a Wife and Widdowe meet on their way to make an offering at the goddess' shrine. When a young maiden appears and places herself at the head of the procession, she offends the older women and precipitates the debate in which each lady extols her own condition as the supreme state of womanhood.

The modest wit of the poem consists primarily in artful statement, sometimes with an almost Baconian pithiness, and in line-capping development of figures of speech, as in the following examples:

WIFE.   The wife is as a Diamond richly set;
MAID.   The maide vnset doth yet more rich appeare.
WIDDOW.   The widdow a Iewel in the Cabinet,
          Which though not worn is stil esteem'd as deare.

                         ❀   ❀   ❀

WIFE.   Wiues are faire houses kept and furnisht well.
WIDDOW.   Widdowes old castles voide, but ful of state;
MAID.   But maids are temples where the Gods do dwell,
          To whom alone themselues they dedicate.

As the exchange continues, the implied compliment to the Virgin Queen becomes more explicit as the Maid gains a victory over her wordy combatants with a speech lauding the state of "spotless maids" and praising "The soueraigne spirit that will be thrall to none" and "The Princely Eagle that still flyes alone." The debate concludes with the three ladies' approaching the goddess and with the Maid's presenting her with their offering, something no doubt more substantial than the verbal praise she had just heard.

With two or three exceptions, Davies' social Muse did not inspire work of abiding literary value. But the pieces we have considered do afford interesting glimpses into the social life of a great age and the integration of poetry into that life in a way scarcely known today. For Davies, such efforts were primarily social gestures, and, except for *Hymnes of Astraea,* not worthy of publication with *Orchestra* and *Nosce Teipsum* in the collection of his work published in 1622. *A Lotterie* and *A Contention* alone would hardly have won Davies the lasting attention and good offices of men like Egerton and Cecil. But his talent to amuse and to entertain, it is reasonable to think, helped keep fresh their awareness of his acute mind and loyal commitment; and his genial wit helped to retain the good will of such patrons.

CHAPTER V

The Religious Verse

IN THIS study of Sir John Davies' poetry, consideration remains to be given to Davies' two principal contributions to the religious literature of his day. The first, *Nosce Teipsum*, "one of the very few permanently readable philosophical poems in English,"[1] is a lengthy dissertation on the nature and immortality of the human soul. The second is his translation, or more correctly, his "metaphrase," of some fifty of the Psalms. That "the English Martial" and the witty dance-master to the universe could direct his talents to such soberly philosophical and meditative writing is yet another manifestation of this young Renaissance gentleman's versatility as a writer and of his breadth of interest. For our more cautiously specialized age, there is a quality of bravura—perhaps presumption—about a young lawyer and political careerist, no more than twenty-eight years old, who understakes to discourse on the nature and immortality of the soul. Such a venture recalls those grand intellectual gestures of a Sir Walter Raleigh's undertaking to write a history of the world or a Sir Francis Bacon's taking all knowledge as his province.

Davies' religious poetry reflects important general cultural interests of the sixteenth century. For students of literature, the English Renaissance is the period of Marlowe, Shakespeare, and the other great dramatists; Spenser and Milton; the lyricists, sonneteers, and "metaphysical" poets. However, the writing of such figures represents a fairly small part of the total number of works issuing in growing profusion from the presses. The sheer mass of religious work published during this period is impressive. Volumes of sermons; how-to devotional manuals offering instruction in prayer, worship, and spiritual discipline, in living a godly (and prosperous) life and in dying a peaceful (and

111

hopeful) death; collections of prayers and meditations for all occasions; translations and excerpts from the Bible, along with numerous aids to its interpretation and better understanding, found their way into the homes, the thoughts, and, presumably, the conduct of thousands upon thousands of Englishmen.[2]

In addition to such prose works, plays dealing with biblical subjects continued to be written and performed; and a considerable body of religious verse was published. Carols for the major festivals in the Christian calendar; verse saints' lives; didactic treatments of such debated topics as the Eucharist, icons, religious vestments, rites and ceremonies; metrical paraphrases of the Scriptures; poems of moral exhortation and doctrinal enlightenment; and verse of a general devotional and meditational nature—for all of these forms the sweet numbers of poetry were enlisted to make religious teachings more palatable.[3]

Much of this verse lacks intrinsic literary merit and requires the special motivations and energies of doctoral researchers to sustain a thorough examination of it. But the modes of thought which it represents and the concerns which it reveals afford useful perspectives on the times in general and on those writers in particular whose merit transcends their own historical periods. *Nosce Teipsum* is much more sophisticated and, in a sense, more learned than most of this writing; and it is addressed to a more educated audience. But it is a part of that widespread religious expression of a period that, as Louis B. Wright has observed, was generally oppressed by "the imminence of eternity" and whose hope of immortality "was still the refuge of a world where human life hung by the frailest of threads."[4] It comes as no surprise, therefore, that *Nosce Teipsum* enjoyed a popularity and high commendation unequaled by any other of Davies' poems.

NOSCE TEIPSUM

I *Date and Occasion*

Following Davies' startling attack on Richard Martin and his subsequent expulsion from the Middle Temple and disbarment from the practice of law, Davies, according to Anthony à Wood,

"retired for a time in private ... and follow'd his studies. ..."[5]
During the winter months of his discontent, he must frequently,
and ruefully, have relived his rash actions and lamented his
damaged professional hopes. But, with leisure to reflect upon
his condition and to order his thoughts, he was able to redeem
the time and, perhaps, his fortunes, among other efforts, by
bringing forward "that excellent philosophical and divine poem
called *Nosce Teipsum*,"[6] which was entered in the *Stationers'
Register* in April of 1599[7] and published in the same year. Its
affirmative reception by the powerful must have greatly sweet-
ened for our poet the reputed uses of adversity.

Some have perhaps overdramatized the composition of this
poem by picturing it as the effusion of "a penitent voluptuary,"
the spontaneous overflow of a powerful and profound spiritual
crisis. Such an almost embarrassingly romanticized view is
proposed by A. B. Grosart: "His great poem bears witness to
very poignant self-accusation and humiliation. Towards the
close you seem to catch the echo of sobs and the glistening of
tears; nor is it 'preaching' to recognize a diviner element still—
his unrest and burden alike laid on Him Who alone can sustain
and help a 'wounded spirit' in its trouble."[8]

That the poem to some degree reflects Davies' recent experiences is certainly suggested by the following passage in Elegy I,
where, commenting upon the instructive uses of "affliction,"
he writes:

> If ought can teach vs ought, *Afflictions* lookes,
>   (Making vs looke into our selues so neere,)
>   Teach vs to *know our selues* beyond all bookes,
>   Or all the learned Schooles that euer were.
>
> This *mistresse* lately pluckt me by the eare,
>   And many a golden lesson hath me taught;
>   Hath made my *Senses* quicke, and Reason cleare,
>   Reform'd my Will and rectified my Thought.
>
> So doe the *winds* and *thunders* cleanse the ayre;
>   So working lees settle and purge the wine;
>   So lop't and pruned trees doe flourish faire;
>   So doth the fire the drossie gold refine.

Neither *Minerua* nor the learned Muse,
　　Nor rules of *Art*, nor *precepts* of the wise;
　　Could in my braine those beames of skill infuse,
　　As but the glance of this Dame's angry eyes.

She within *lists* my ranging minde hath brought,
　　That now beyond my selfe I list not goe;
　　My selfe am *center* of my circling thought,
　　Onely *my selfe* I studie, learne, and know.[9]

Among the golden lessons Davies learned from this stern
schoolmistress were better governance of his energies and avoid-
ance of recklessness; at least his successful career in Ireland,
soon to be begun, reflected self-discipline and singleness of
purpose in a marked degree. But in recent years students, who
have qualified the view of *Nosce Teipsum* as the expression
of a humble and contrite heart, have suggested that Davies'
piety was not a little tempered by a rather realistic expediency.
A show of thoughtful, sober, soundly orthodox, no-nonsense
religious and philosophical views might well have served to
regain for the poet the confidence and, better yet, the intercessory powers of those able to advance his career. Such a
view, perhaps, may owe too much to the cynicism of our own
time; a cautious and historical charity might suggest that behind
the publication of the poem at this particular point lay what
made it both desirable and necessary: a chastened spirit and
a hopeful ambition.

The composition of *Nosce Teipsum* is usually dated during
Davies' retirement, but there is reason to think that a significant
part of the work had actually been written some years earlier.
The evidence for an earlier date of composition merits consideration.[10] On what authority the dedicatory verses to Queen
Elizabeth in William Ravenhill's edition of *Nosce Teipsum* in
1689 and in that of Nahum Tate's in 1697 were dated July 11,
1592, is now unknown. This date also appears in British Museum
Add. MS. 25304, p. 2, a late seventeenth-century manuscript,
which preserves a transcription of the poem. Grosart rejected
this date as lacking authority and as contradicting "all the
known facts and circumstances."[11] But one or two items seem
to support its possible validity. First, although the "Carte

Notes" contain some errors of fact and actually associate the composition of the poem with Davies' rustication following his attack on Martin, they also describe *Nosce Teipsum* as "yᵉ first essay of Davies' pen,"[12] thereby disturbing the usually accepted chronology of Davies' work.

If *Nosce Teipsum* was, indeed, the "first" piece of Davies' writing, the date of 1592 would seem an appropriate one in relation to the known or likely dates of his other works. Second, and more significant, what would seem to be an early reference to the poem appears in Thomas Nashe's "Dedicatorie" to *Strange Newes,* published in 1592: "By what soeuer thy visage holdeth most pretious I beseech thee, by Iohn Dauies soule and the blew Bore in the Spittle, I coniure thee, to draw out thy purse, and giue me nothing for the dedication of my Pamphlet."[13] While it is possible that Nashe is alluding to some Davies other than our poet, and perhaps attaching some significance to "soule" other than an allusion to Davies' poem, it seems more likely that "Iohn Dauies soule" is, as R. B. McKerrow suggests, a reference to *Nosce Teipsum.* Noting that the poem was not published until 1599, McKerrow thinks Nashe was probably referring "to some early version of the poem which had been circulated in MS."[14]

Challenging this early date, however, are certain complimentary passages in Elegy II of *Nosce Teipsum* which refer to Davies' patron Sir Thomas Egerton. In comparing the relationship between the soul and its function in the gathering of sense data to a judge and his eliciting evidence from witnesses, Davies writes of the man

> . . . whom she [Elizabeth] doth now aduance,
> Vpon her gracious *mercy-seat* to sit;
> Doth common things, of course and circumstance,
> To the reports of common men commit:

> But when the cause it selfe must be decreed,
> Himselfe in person, in his proper Court,
> To graue and solemne hearing doth proceed,
> Of euery proofe and euery by-report.

> Then, like God's angell he pronounceth right,
> And milke and hony from his tongue doth flow;

> Happie are they that still are in his sight,
> To reape the wisedome which his lips doe sow.[15]

A marginal gloss in the 1602 edition of the poem identifies Sir Thomas Egerton as the individual referred to, whom Elizabeth had advanced to the "mercy-seat" as her Lord Chancellor in May of 1596.

A possible resolution of these conflicting dates may be effected if we assume that *Nosce Teipsum* is a product of accretion, revision, and, possibly, adaptation. What is now Elegy II, "Of the Soule of Man and the Immortalitie Thereof," is probably the work referred to by Nashe. It seems to be the most indebted to "sources" and the most derivative of all Davies' poems, suggesting early work and possibly work completed during or shortly after his years at Oxford. Circulated in manuscript, the poem may have come to Nashe's attention in the early 1590's. With time on his hands during his retreat from London, Davies may have returned to this poem, added the stanzas which compliment Egerton and what is now Elegy I, "Of Humane Knowledge," which contains the stanzas of more immediately personal implication and relevance to the poet's recent encounter with affliction, and prepared the work for publication.[16]

Such a view of the poem's composition, of course, qualifies the older notion of Davies as a humble penitent who distilled from the tears of his distress the artful quatrains of *Nosce Teipsum*. That the completed poem assumed a more pragmatic mission is suggested by the "Carte Notes" in which is recorded Lord Mountjoy's pleasure with the poem and his urging Davies to publish it with a dedication to the Queen. Happily, Davies followed Mountjoy's recommendation, dedicating the poem to his "Dread Soveraigne" and signing it "Her Maiestie's least and vnworthiest Subiect." Davies' hopes must have been considerably brightened when Mountjoy introduced him to Elizabeth, thereby giving him an opportunity to present her with a copy of the poem. According to the "Carte Notes," this "first essay of his pen was so well rellisht y^{tt} ye Queen encouraged him in his studdyes promising him preferment & had him sworn her servant in Ordinary."[17] As earlier indicated, special manuscript copies of the poem were sent to Edward

Cooke, the attorney general, and to the Earl of Northumberland, men who seemed to have befriended the poet in his difficulties. Anthony à Wood records what must have been an exceedingly gratifying experience, and a witness to the power of the poetic word, when Davies was presented to James in Scotland in 1603:

Upon the death of Q. Elizabeth, [Davies], with the lord Hunsdon, went into Scotland to congratulate K. James as her lawful successor; and being introduced into his presence, the king enquired the names of those gentlemen who were in the company of the said lord, and he naming John Davies among, who stood behind them, the king straitway asked, whether he was *Nosce Teipsum?* and being answered that he was the same, he graciously embraced him, and thenceforth had so great a favour for him, that soon after [in 1603] he made him his solicitor and then his attorney-general in Ireland.[18]

It seems quite clear that *Nosce Teipsum,* whatever it may have meant personally to Davies' self-study, is another example of the poet's pen serving to advertise himself and to win the good opinion of those in authority, thereby hoping to improve his situation. While assuredly differing in tone and significance of achievement, *Nosce Teipsum,* as G. A. Wilkes suggests,[19] has much in common with the *Hymnes of Astraea, A Lotterie,* and *A Contention*—works which looked to the poet's promotion and career advancement.

II Context and Sources

"Nosce Teipsum" ("Know Thyself") in the title of Davies' poem has an ancient history in Western thought as a maxim attributed to Chilon of Sparta, one of the Seven Sages; and it was one of the inscriptions on the temple at Delphi. The theme of self-knowledge received memorable statement and development in Classical philosophy and literature, in which the cryptic words of the maxim were made to yield a number of interpretations. To "know one's self" was construed to learn what one can and cannot do as an individual and to discover one's special talents or essential qualities. It could also mean to determine one's human limitations; that is, to know one's place in the larger scheme of life, the limits of human knowledge and wisdom, and the certain brevity of man's life. In the *Tusculan Disputations,* Cicero construed the maxim in a way suggestive of Davies' poem, namely, to know one's *soul.* Among the Neo-Platonists, the knowledge of one's soul, as with Davies, involved a psychological analysis of the soul's faculties and functions. The maxim was easily adaptable to Christian thought and spiritual discipline; but the pursuit of self-knowledge in this tradition revealed one's sinful state, one's kinship with God, the hope of eternal life, and the possibility of eternal damnation.

During the sixteenth century, statements and developments of the *nosce* theme appeared both in secular and in religious contexts. We encounter it in the writings of Erasmus, Thomas Elyot, Roger Ascham, Montaigne, and Bacon, where it appears as a caution against pride and as a recommendation that man learn to gauge his capacities and to find his proper place in the order of creation. The theme of self-knowledge is developed at some length in the religious writing of Luther and Calvin, where the focus is primarily on the knowledge of the human soul, its sinful state, and its need for redemption.[20]

An interesting formulation of the *nosce* theme in a religious context occurs in *The French Academie* of Pierre de la Primaudaye. This massive and influential work, first published in Paris in 1577 and translated into English in 1594, was a popular encyclopedic compendium of Renaissance thought. As we shall see later, Davies seems to have drawn upon this work in writing *Nosce Teipsum.* Concerning the theme of self-knowledge, Primaudaye writes:

. . . that sentence which saith, *Knowe thy selfe,* was not without good reason so much praised and renowned amongst al the ancient Greeke and Latin philosophers, as that which is worthy to be taken for a heauenly oracle, and a sentence pronounced by the mouth of God. For whosoeuer shall know himselfe well, cannot faile to know God his creator, and to honour him as he ought, if he follow the chiefe end for which man was created, as well as the residue of the creatures. . . . For although the knowlege of the rest of the creatures that are in this visible worlde, will greatly helpe to leade him to the knowledge of God the Creatour, neuerthelesse he shall neuer be able to know him well, if withall he know not himselfe. Yea these two knowledges are so ioyned togither, that it is a very hard matter to seuer them. For as a man can not know himselfe if he know not God, so he cannot know God wel, if in like sort he know not himselfe. So that I take this for most certain that neither Astronomy, Geometry, Geography, or Cosmography, nor any other Mathematical science is so necessary for man, as that wherby he may learne to know himselfe wel, and to measure himselfe wel by the measure of his owne nature, that he may thereby know how to contayne himselfe within the limits thereof.[21]

Within the larger context of general religious writings, Primaudaye's *French Academie* and Davies' *Nosce Teipsum*, as well as poems like John Davies of Hereford's *Microcosmos* and Fulke Greville's verse treatise *Of Human Learning*, have more specific purposes—to refute the "libertine" and "Epicurean" atheistical thought which increasingly began to challenge important tenets of the Christian faith during the sixteenth century.[22] The growth of such views seems to have owed something to the divisiveness within the church itself and to its splintering into numerous sects and factions; for the different versions of the "truth" raised serious questions for many concerning which version, if any, was the true one. Richard Hooker was one of several writers who related the growth of atheistical thought to the controversy within the church. In Book V (1597) of *The Laws of Ecclesiastical Polity*, he wrote:

With our contentions their [the atheists'] irreligious humour is also much strengthened. Nothing pleaseth them better than these manifold oppositions upon the matter of religion, as for that they have hereby the more opportunity to learn on one side how the other may be oppugned, and so to weaken the credit of all unto themselves; as also because of this hot pursuit of lower controversies among men professing religion, and agreeing in the principal foundations thereof, they conceive hope about the higher principles themselves time will cause altercation to grow.[23]

Questioning of traditional religious beliefs was probably also abetted by the study of such Classical pagan writers as Lucian, Lucretius, and Cicero, who in various ways—sometimes sardonic, sometimes deeply philosophical—challenged attitudes and assumptions found in most forms of religious thought, pagan or

Christian. However misinterpreted and imperfectly understood, the political writings of Machiavelli—which sanctioned the displacement of traditional Christian values and ethical teachings by a pragmatic expediency—forcefully supported a vision of life unencumbered with the restraints of Christian discipline. As the ferment of ideas developed during the Renaissance and as the old intellectual containers were increasingly strained to accommodate new and revolutionary concepts and discoveries, "new philosophy," in Donne's famous formulation, must have called all things in doubt for many.

The publication of works inimical to the Christian faith could be dangerous for the authors and publishers alike, a fact which probably accounts for the scarcity of such works. But that disbelief in cherished ideas like the existence of God, personal immortality, and the atonement and resurrection of Christ was growing is evidenced by the number of defenses of such beliefs which began to appear in this period, not only in sermons but also in various religious treatises attacking disbelievers and defending Christian tenets.

As early as 1530, John Rastell in his *New Boke of Purgatory* undertook to refute the contentions of unbelievers by rational arguments. His book consists of three dialogues: the first and the third seek to establish the existence of God and purgatory, respectively; the third, employing arguments similar to Davies', seeks to prove the immortality of the individual soul.[24] Some years later, Bishop John Woolton published *The Immortalitie of the Soul* (1576); but the Bishop was less hopeful than Rastell that the soul's immortality could be demonstrated by purely rational arguments and depended upon scriptural teachings to support his views. He did, however, include some reasoned arguments relating to the soul, which anticipated some of Davies' verse arguments.[25]

Another French treatise, akin in purpose to that of *The French Academie*, was Philip Mornay's *A worke concerning the trunesse of the Christian religion against Atheists, Epicures, Paynims, Jewes, Mahumetists, and other Infidels*, first published in Antwerp in 1581 and translated into English by Sir Philip Sidney and Arthur Golding in 1587. This work, popular in England, is pointedly directed to controverting religious disbelief. Of particular interest for *Nosce Teipsum* is chapter fourteen, entitled "That the Soule of man is immortall, or dieth not," upon which Davies seems to have drawn for part of Elegy II of *Nosce Teipsum*.[26]

That *Nosce Teipsum*, too, was a document growing out of the religious controversy of this period seems clear. In Elegy II, the poet directly addresses "these light and vicious persons" who regard the soul as so much "smoake, or ayrie blast."[27] And the objections to the belief in the soul's immortality which Davies states and refutes are attributed to "impious wits," "Epicures," and "vaine spirits."[28] To assist him in silencing the disbelieving, Davies made use of ancient, traditional, widely approved arguments and, as is quite likely, the works of Mornay and Primaudaye.

Davies' admiring editor, A. B. Grosart, valued *Nosce Teipsum* for its "deep and original thought"[29]; and he angrily dismissed as "absolutely untrue, an utter delusion," a notion put forward by Alexander Dalrymple that the poem was chiefly taken from *The Nature of Man* by Nemesius, the early Church Father and Bishop of Emesa in Syria.[30] Despite Grosart's assurances of Davies' independent thought, a number of students have carefully worked through the poem and traced many of its ideas to a host of thinkers, thereby effectively dispelling any claim Davies might have had as an "original thinker." There is little agreement among such students on *the* source Davies utilized; and the non-specialist in the history of Western religious thought, overwhelmed by their confident erudition, tends to be convinced by the last scholar he has read. In a very useful study of the poem, E. H. Sneath, unlike Grosart, is certain "that Nemesius was one of the predecessors whom Davies had consulted with advantage," as were Aristotle, Cicero, and Calvin.[31] Margarete Seemann, who discounts the influence of Nemesius, cites a large number of parallel passages and finds Davies' principal indebtedness to be to Aristotle and to such commentators upon him as St. Thomas Aquinas.[32] Additional studies of the poem have produced more candidates as "sources"; the growing list includes Plato, Galen, the Bible, Lactantius, St. Augustine, Plotinus, Cornelius Agrippa, Henry Bullinger, Melancthon, and Timothy Bright. No doubt more names will be proposed as students find other writers who responded to an ancient tradition of beliefs in much the same way as Davies did.

Such an *embarrass de richesses* in sources might suggest, however, that Davies was not indebted to *a* source but was reflecting a complex of traditional, almost commonplace, ideas about the soul, human psychology, and the existence of God. We might well expect a university-trained man like Davies to have been exposed to many of the authors mentioned above, particularly to the Classical figures; but it does not seem necessary to insist that he deliberately consulted such writers as Aristotle, Nemesius, or St. Augustine in order to write his poem. In the sixteenth century, many employed neo-Platonic ideas which were currently in vogue without having read Plato or his followers, just as today many talk and write easily of the id, ego, and superego, repression, and sublimation without having felt the necessity to read Freud.

But especially convincing cases have been made by Louis I. Bredvold and by George T. Buckley for Davies' direct use of Philip Mornay's *Trunesse of the Christian religion* and Pierre de la Primaudaye's *French Academie*.[33] The similarities in purpose, plan, idea, and details between Davies' poem and these two works, as noted by these scholars, strongly argue for their influence on Davies. Bredvold notes a number of significant parallels between Primaudaye's and Davies' discussion of psychology.[34] Although conceding that these parallels "do in many cases preclude the possibility of doubt" concerning Davies' indebtedness to Primaudaye, Buckley contends that Davies also incorporated significant material from Mornay's volume; and he makes a strong case for his view in comparing Davies' discussion of the immortality of the soul with that of Mornay.[35] One example from the many which he cites has to suffice here. Arguing that the soul retains its powers, although the senses become weakened by age or illness, Davies writes:

> So, when the body serues her turne no more,
>   And all her *Senses* are extinct and gone,
>   She can discourse of what she learn'd before,
>   In heauenly contemplations, all alone.

one, by denigrating man's intellectual pride and scoring the vanity of his busy pursuit of knowledge; and, two, by directing man to an inward view and knowledge of himself.

The depreciation of man's ability to know and the validity of what he takes to be true knowledge has ancient Classical and Christian roots.[38] Classical skepticism grew from the teachings and scattered sayings of Pyrrho and their formulation by Sextus Empiricus and was further developed by Cicero in the *Academic Questions*. The vanity of worldly knowledge was also voiced by St. Paul and St. Augustine. In the Renaissance, this view was given expression by the German Humanist Heinrich Cornelius Agrippa in *Of the Vanitie and vncertaintie of Artes and Sciences*, first published in Antwerp in 1531 and several times translated into English during the sixteenth century. In this popular work, Agrippa satirizes the current state of knowledge and ridicules the confusions of the academicians.

A more darkly sceptical poem, perhaps contemporary in composition with Davies' *Nosce Teipsum,* is Fulke Greville's *Treati[s]e of Human Learning*, published posthumously in 1633, which denies the validity of sense perception and of human reason as means of knowing the truth. Perhaps the most sustained attack on man's capacity to know is Montaigne's long essay *An Apology for Raymond Sebonde;* and much of Montaigne's castigation of man's presumption and intellectual pride suggests Davies' attitudes in Elegy I. Montaigne's skepticism afforded a soft pillow upon which to lay a head weary of thought, for it encouraged the view that religious truth was a matter to be accepted on faith. But Davies' view of man's proneness to error and his inability to find truth outside himself led him not to forsake the pursuit of knowledge but to restrict the scope of human inquiry to the contemplation of what, with God's grace, he could hope to understand—himself. *Nosce Teipsum* seeks to direct human reasoning toward such an exploration.

The ideas of Elegy I are developed in a clear, orderly sequence colored by the personal experiences of the poet and punctuated with an emotionally heightened concluding pronouncement on the human estate.[39] The pursuit of knowledge was what had led Adam and Eve to sin; their sinful aspiration

to know resulted not only in their disobedience of God but
also in the impairment of their reason:

> Where they sought *knowledge*, they did *error* find;
> Ill they desir'd to know, and ill they did;
> And to giue *Passion* eyes, made *Reason* blind.[40]

Their Reason darkened and they no longer,

> Could the faire formes of *Good* and *Truth* discern;
> *Battes* they became that *eagles* were before;
> And this they got by their *desire to learne*.[41]

Davies thus develops a Calvinistic view of an "intellectual Fall"
as well as a spiritual one.[42]

As the unfortunate offspring of Adam and Eve, we inherit
both their "fond fruitless curiositie" to "seeke for knowledge
hid" and the inability ever adequately to satisfy that restless
curiosity. Our quests for knowledge prove illusory and delud-
ing, even fatal to our best interests, as in the examples of
Phaethon's aspiring to drive the sun chariot and Icarus' soaring
too high above the earth. Our efforts to know and discern are
doomed, for what can we hope to know,

> When *Error* chokes the windoes of the minde,
> The diuers formes of things, how can we learne,
> That haue been euer from our birth-day blind?
>
> When *Reasone's* lampe, which (like the *sunne* in skie)
> Throughout *Man's* little world her beames did spread;
> Is now become a sparkle, which doth lie
> Vnder the ashes, halfe extinct, and dead:
>
> How can we hope, that through the eye and eare,
> This dying sparkle, in this cloudy place,
> Can recollect these beames of knowledge cleere,
> Which were infus'd in the first minds by grace?[43]

We err, thus, in seeking knowledge of the external; what is
of prime importance is still within our competence—self-

knowledge. But we resist such a personal exploration because of the unflattering image we gain of ourselves; we are frightened by the ugliness we perceive, as in the ancient fable the unnatural Io,

> Which for her lust was turned into a cow;
> When thirstie to a streame she did repaire,
> And saw her selfe transform'd she wist not how:
>
> At first she startles, then she stands amaz'd,
>   At last with terror she from thence doth flye;
>   And loathes the watry glasse wherein she gaz'd
>   And shunnes it still, though she for thirst doe die:
>
> Euen so *Man's Soule* which did God's image beare,
>   And was at first faire, good, and spotlesse pure;
>   Since with her *sinnes* her beauties blotted were,
>   Doth of all sights her owne sight least endure.[44]

Sometimes Affliction can so forcefully strike us that we are compelled to an inward contemplation, a withdrawal into ourselves in which "The *Minde* contracts her selfe and shrinketh in, / And to her selfe she gladly doth retire,"

> As *Spiders* toucht, seek their webs inmost part;
>   As *bees* in stormes vnto their hiues returne;
>   As bloud in danger gathers to the heart;
>   As men seek towns, when foes the country burn.[45]

Such has been the recent experience of the poet from which he has learned a "golden lesson," one which, he reports, "Hath made my *Senses* quicke, and Reason cleare, / Reform'd my Will and rectifide my Thought."[46] And the fruits of this refreshed sensitivity and renewed understanding are formulated in the justly famous and moving climax of the first Elegy:

> I know my bodie's of so fraile a kind,
>   As force without, feauers within can kill;
>   I know the heauenly nature of my minde,
>   But 'tis corrupted both in wit and will:

I know my *Soule* hath power to know all things,
Yet is she blinde and ignorant in all;
I know I am one of Nature's little kings,
Yet to the least and vilest things am thrall.

I know my life's a paine and but a span,
I know my *Sense* is mockt with euery thing:
And to conclude, I know my selfe a MAN,
Which is a *proud,* and yet a *wretched* thing.[47]

Elegy I is, in its own right, a satisfying poem; and the modern reader can easily participate in its vision. With sufficient variety to avoid monotony, the sombre quatrains move in a solemn cadence to the climactic revelation of MAN as a *"proud,* and yet a *wretched* thing,"* a climax both logically and rhetorically congruent: logically, as an outcome of the exploration of "humane knowledge"; rhetorically, as appropriate to the emotional significance of that discovery. There is also an agreeable surprise about the conclusion as the reader perceives in Davies' personal experience a universal significance; that to a degree the "self" which the poet has come to know is a part of Everyman.

While we find artful statement and lucid exposition in Elegy II, as well as emotionally alive passages, interest sometimes flags amid "proofs," "objections," and "answers to objections"; and we recall Edgar Allan Poe's insistence that there is no such thing as a long poem. The reader's attention is also sometimes distracted by his disagreement with this argument or that, or he is embarrassed by the poet's occasional question-begging and logical lapses. In contrast, Elegy I satisfies in that it is large enough to permit a sufficiently complex exploration of its theme, to incorporate pagan legend within Christian history, and to relate the poet's individual experience to other men's; nonetheless, it is sufficiently limited to maintain the reader's alert attention and continued interest.

The poem's argument and mood draw strength from a tension of opposed, sometimes paradoxical, conceptions: the aspirations of Man (whether as Adam, Prometheus, Phaethon, or Icarus) and the calamity of his Fall; his proud vision of himself and his

wretched state; his Reason, once like the sun spreading beams
"Throughout *Man's* little world," now "a sparkle" lying "Vnder
the ashes, halfe extinct, and dead"; his soul which once "did
God's image beare" "at first faire, good, and spotlesse pure," now
"blotted" with sin; and "the wisest of all mortall men," knowing
only that he did not know.

Elegy I speaks the language of the late sixteenth-century
England, and its ideas reach backward in time; but it projects a
vision of man quickly recognized by many in the present century.

IV   *Elegy II. "Of the Soule of Man,*
and the immortalitie thereof."

Elegy I has memorably posed the unresolved problem: Man
stultified by his contradictions and tormented by his restless
anxiety. As an answer, in language remarkable for its clarity
and condensation of thought, and drawing upon ideas which had
been current in Europe for centuries, Elegy II offers a vision of
man's harmonious integration of his physical and spiritual powers
and an ecstatically joyful confidence in his heavenly destiny.

The opening stanzas restate the theme of man's intellectual
limitations enunciated in Elegy I: Man's eyes may tell him something of the world about him, but they "looke not into this little
world" of self. The vanity of past human efforts to think to any
significant conclusion concerning man's inner being is manifested
in the conflicting and sometimes frivolous views proposed by
"Great Wits" concerning the nature and location of the soul.
But the poet is certain that his inquiry will produce valid results,
for God has given him, as He gave St. Augustine, "an *inward
light*," whose power he invokes to illumine his spirit. Although
man suffered an intellectual darkening as a consequence of his
Fall, God's grace, as it affords him the opportunity of redemption, also renews the power of his mind. The "bright Morning
Star" of God's grace

> ... in these later times hast brought to light
> Those mysteries, that since the world begun,
> Lay hid in darknesse, and eternall night:

> Thou (*like the sunne*) dost with indifferent ray,
> Into the *palace* and the *cottage* shine,

And shew'st the *soule* both to the clerke and lay,
By the cleare *lampe* of Thy *Oracle* diuine.

This Lampe through all the regions of my braine,
Where my *soule* sits, doth spread such beames of grace,
As now, me thinks, I do distinguish plain,
Each subtill line of her immortall face.[48]

Confident that he can delineate his soul's "immortal face,"
Davies sets about doing so, grouping his ideas under two principal subjects: first, a dissertation on the nature of the soul and
its mode of existence and interaction with the body; and, second,
a presentation of arguments for its immortality. Each of these
sections is concluded by an "Acclamation," an emotionally
charged, prayer-like celebration of the truth which has been
revealed by God's grace.

Davies develops his definition of the soul as a spiritual substance—that is, an immaterial essence—with an individuality of
its own. He counters the views that would deny the soul's spiritual
status, and views that would explain the soul's being and opera-
tions as mere forms of sensation or as manifestations of the
body's "humours"—the blood, black and yellow bile, and phlegm,
which in the physiology of the day constituted man's physical
make-up. Likewise, he discounts the materialistic notion which
would identify the soul and body as one and the same. The
soul, he insists,

. . . is a *substance*, and a reall thing,
Which hath it selfe an actuall working might;
Which neither from the Senses' power doth spring,
Nor from the bodie's humors, tempred right.[49]

After a consideration of the origin of the soul and its mode
of interaction with the body, Davies analyzes into three groups
the principal "powers" which the soul possesses: the "Vegetatiue
or Quickening Powers," the "Powers of Sense," and the "Intellectual Powers of the Soule." The first group energizes man's
being and operates his faculties; the second, which Davies develops at considerable length, is divided into "apprehensive"
powers and "motive" powers. Apprehensive powers include the

"outward" senses of sight, hearing, taste, smell, and feeling, and "inward" senses of "Common Sense," "Fantasie," and "Memorie," which process data supplied by the outward senses. Motive powers embrace the "Passions of Sense"—the emotions of joy, grief, fear, hope, hate, and love—and the "vitall spirits," which moving through the arteries "Continuall motion to all parts doe bring." The principal intellectual powers are Wit and Will, which

> . . . the nature of the *Soule declare,*
> For to man's *soule* these onely proper bee;
> For on the Earth no other wights there are
> That haue these heauenly powers, but only we.[50]

Wit analyzes and interprets sense data which she finds in "the mirror of the Fantasie," makes abstractions from them, understands causes and their effects, evaluates, reasons "from ground to ground" to conclusions, forms opinions, and makes judgments. Will is the power to choose and to commit a man to action; it interacts closely with Wit, and

> . . . puts in practice what the *Wit* deuiseth:
> *Will* euer acts, and *Wit* contemplates still;
> And as from *Wit*, the power of *wisedome* riseth,
> *All other vertues* daughters are of *Will*.[51]

Davies' orderly presentation has moved from body to mind, from the lowest of the soul's powers to the highest. Following a summary, which pictures the close harmony and marvels at the integration of the soul's three powers, the "Acclamation" extolls the greatness of God's work in giving man a soul:

> O! what a liuely life, what heauenly power,
>   What spreading vertue, what a sparkling fire!
> How great, how plentifull, how rich a dower
>   Dost Thou within this dying flesh inspire![52]

The "Acclamation" markedly contrasts with the vision of man as "a *proud,* and yet a *wretched* thing" developed in Elegy I. "Nosce Teipsum" has been validated, knowledge of self has revealed treasures of man's hope and God's love unknown to those whose view is outward and whose mental darkness is not illuminated by God's light.

The climax of Elegy II is the assertion of the soul's immortality, which Davies supports by six traditional "reasons" or arguments, and which he defends against five equally traditional objections. As an example of these arguments, the first may be mentioned. Man has a desire for knowledge—"To *learne* and *know the truth* of euery thing"—a desire which is an essential quality of the soul. His brief stay on earth does not permit him to satisfy this desire, and God would not have given him this appetite had he not intended him to satisfy it. Accordingly, since in this mortal life,

> . . . no *soule* the truth can know
> So perfectly, as it hath power to doe;
> If then perfection be not found below,
> An higher place must make her mount thereto.[53]

Moving toward the final Acclamation, Davies draws together many of the threads of the arguments developed throughout Elegy II in a section headed "Three Kinds of Life answerable to the three Powers of the Soule." Prior to birth, the soul's quickening powers prevail; following birth, the powers of sense become dominant. As the child matures, Reason begins to manifest itself; and the soul aspires to leave the body and to enter a third and unending life, the life of Reason, when man "shall of God enioy the reall sight." The Acclamation that closes the poem exhorts Man to cultivate the beauties of his soul, to have no fear of death, and to be humble before God's glory.

Nosce Teipsum was extremely popular in its own time. Not only did it win the favor of the great, like Mountjoy, Elizabeth, and James, but also it was well received by the general public. It appeared in six editions during Davies' lifetime and was frequently reprinted thereafter.[54] For the student of late sixteenth-century life, it affords one of the clearest available statements of conventional and orthodox thought about man's psychology and his eternal prospects. It seems almost designed to supply illustrations for scholars like Tillyard and Theodore Spencer in depicting the elements of the Elizabethan world view. Notions of order and hierarchical organization are apparent in the poem's very structure and appear in the familiar metaphors of the chain of being, the correspondence between macrocosm and microcosm, and the musical symbolism. In short, as Felix E. Schelling observed, "*Nosce Teipsum* is as typical a representative of Elizabethan popular philosophy as the *Essay on Man* is typical of the popular thought of the time of Queen Anne...."[55]

While Davies' poem has unmistakable historical interest, its overt didacticism offends, even bores, many modern readers. It is unlikely that many will find Davies' thought either convincing or distinguished. Setting aside the outmoded psychology and physiology, we feel that Davies' arguments for the immortality of the soul and for the existence of God are more often pat verbalizations of foregone convictions unaccountably arrived at than thorough-going rational proofs. And we are occasionally annoyed that from such slender arguments Davies can derive such confidence and certainty. His intellectual swagger is excessive in terms of the force of his thought. Too frequently, pious assertions take the place of proof, assumptions turn up to justify conclusions, and wish-fulfillment is disguised as genuine argument.

But the certainties of one age frequently appear as naive to a later time, and perhaps ultimately all such metaphysical speculations are equally naive or equally valid. The poem merits our intellectual respect because of the significant questions which it seriously seeks to answer. Final answers concerning most of the mysteries of human consciousness and mental functions remain to be heard, and the yearning to make sense out of human existence and destiny still nags, drawing together all ages in a common bafflement. Viewed from a perspective of three hundred years, the poem takes on a touching, even a poignant, quality, as Davies attempts to assert a victorious vision of man against the darkness and defeat of death. We can admire his refusal to accept a dusty answer to his urgent questioning about man's destiny; and we can be moved at his human capacity to think that what he wished were true was so. "If death do quench vs quite, we haue great wrong," he writes. It is a plaintive cry that sounds throughout the poem—one which Davies' most cheerful assertions never quite silence for us.

V *Style, Unity, and Form*

If T. S. Eliot found Davies' theories limited and superficial, he expressed nonetheless considerable admiration for *Nosce Teipsum* as a poem.[56] Eliot found its merit and interest to "reside in the perfection of the instrument to the end."[57] Esthetic pleasure is provided by the poem's carefully ordered argument and by its structure, which cumulatively builds in both rational sequence and emotional importance from the opening to the concluding lines; in the artfully controlled vocabulary, images, and figures; and in its language which has the lucidity of good prose and the melody and heightened emotional tone of verse.

Many have praised Davies' skill in handling the difficult decasyllabic quatrain. As a poet, Davies seems to have thrived on formal restraints. As he mastered the rhyme royal stanzas of *Orchestra* and the acrostic patterns of the *Hymnes*, he masters the quatrain here. There is enough metric and rhythmic variation to avoid monotony in so long a poem; throughout the four hundred or more stanzas, in Theodore Spencer's words, never do "the demands of the argument deaden the verse" or "the demands of the verse obscure the argument."[58] Expounding the ideas in independent quatrains assists the reader's grasp of the poem's development, and the momentum of argument provides a continuity instead of a brick pile of isolated ideas.

The careful building of his argument is the principal source of unity in *Nosce Teipsum*, but for some readers the marked contrasts in mood and idea between Elegies I and II disturb the poem's unity. To these readers, the two Elegies seem almost like two discrete, independent poems related only because Davies, by publishing them together under a common title, implied they were. While the contrasts do exist, and it is quite possible that the two Elegies come from different periods of composition, in my judgment *Nosce Teipsum* has artistic unity.

Davies has unified the two principal parts of the poem in several ways. First, the two Elegies are related as complementary explorations of a Christian version of the *nosce* theme. In Elegy I, the poet learns to study himself, as opposed to the vain and distractive world about him; but that study reveals his fallen and painfully paradoxical state—that of a proud and yet a wretched creature aspiring to knowledge but finding only error, one of Nature's little kings, yet the slave to "the least and vilest things." It is, however, this intolerable awareness of himself as limited and as despairing that gives impetus to the quest recorded in Elegy II, a quest which with the grace of God's inner light is triumphantly realized. John Davies is not John Donne. Clear statement and argument brought to a firm conclusion are Davies' interests, not the witty exploration of the conceit and the play of paradox on one's sensibility which stimulated Donne. But there is something of Donne's sense of paradox in the relationship between the two Elegies: that he might rise to contemplate eternal life with the intellectual clarity in Elegy II, the poet is first thrown down into confused despair in Elegy I; that he might *know*, he first must learn that he does *not* know.

Davies also unites the two Elegies by employing the same speaker in both, a distinctly individual, human presence who is more than a mouthpiece for a sequence of ideas. In Elegy I, the speaker questions his parents' purpose in sending him to the schools, comments on the golden lessons taught him by Affliction, and laments the discovery of his darkened self in the dramatic series of sentences couched in the first person that conclude the Elegy. In Elegy II, the "I" of the poem gives witness to God's inner light, argues with the "impious wits" and "Epicures" who would mock his belief in the soul's immortality with their trivial "objections," and personalizes the significance of his knowledge of psychology, physiology, and textbook proofs for the existence of God in the two emotional Acclamations. Davies has given *Nosce Teipsum* the semblance of a man thinking: in Elegy I, to an agonizing despair; in Elegy II, to grateful and joyous certitude.

Nosce Teipsum is unified in still other ways. It is a "religious" work not only in its surface "content" but also in its incorporating the principal stages of religious conversion, an intellectual conversion, in the structure of its argument. The speaker first undergoes a conviction of his intellectual "sin" and an awareness of need; this state is followed by a sense of illumination from which he gains a deeper and more meaningful understanding of his soul. Finally, he understands his soul's eternal and heavenly

destiny. *Nosce Teipsum* is Davies' divine comedy, the allegory
of a mind's pilgrimage from a hell of doubt through the purgatory
of intellectual discipline and the purification of understanding,
into the paradisal assurance of eternal life and joy in the company and contemplation of God.

Beneath the "plot" of ideas can also be discerned a comedic
structure which is remarkably similar in movement and outcome
to the archetypal, mythic pattern of comedy which Northrop
Frye has discerned and analyzed.[59] This pattern, according to
Frye, is a version of the nature myth of summer's triumph over
winter, of life over death; and in dramatic form it involves a
movement from one kind of social order to a more desirable
one—from a society in which people imperfectly understand
themselves and their relationship with others to one more near
human longing and desire, in which the contradictions within a
character give way to integration, and the distorted to true self-
knowledge, in which strife and cross-purposes are displaced
by the joys of harmonious relationship. Something very like this
pattern of feeling underlies the experience of the speaker in
Nosce Teipsum. He is aware of his fallen state in Elegy I, of
his loss of harmony and his confused thought. Through a series
of arguments, counterarguments, and replies, Elegy II displaces
the mood of the opening Elegy and prepares man for his enjoyment of God and the society of angels in the heaven toward
which his soul is destined. An eternal summer has overcome the
winter of Elegy I.

Perhaps it is this deep emotional sub-structure that has so stimulated readers' imaginations in the past and that has accounted
significantly for the appeal of *Nosce Teipsum* in its long history.
The "truth" revealed by the poem is, after all, not an intellectual
but an emotional one. Beneath the surface of arguments and
proofs is a more powerful dialectic of emotional need and satisfaction which emerges in the "acclamations" proclaiming a
deliverance from alienation, doubt, and despair and a restoration of belonging, confidence, and hope. Perhaps this voicing
of the heart's need is what T. S. Eliot had in mind when he
wrote concerning *Nosce Teipsum*: "Thought is not exploited for
the sake of feeling, it is pursued for its own sake; and the feeling
is a kind of by-product worth far more than the thought."[60]

VI *Metaphrase of the Psalms*

Anthony à Wood mentioned a *"Metaphrase of several of K. David's Psalms"* as being among some of Davies' manuscripts "which go from hand to hand."[61] But not until late in the nineteenth century was a text of these metrical translations recovered and published. A. B. Grosart found them in a manuscript belonging to David Laing, which contained some minor verse attributed to Davies; and, principally on the basis of internal evidence, he published them in his edition of Davies' poetry in 1876.[62] Headed "The Psalms translated into verse, Anno Domini 1624," they include Psalms 1–50, 67, 91, 95, 100, 103, and 150. Grosart notes that the first fifty are in the handwriting of one of Davies' secretaries. Because the remainder are in a different hand and are separated in the manuscript from the others, he is less confident that they are Davies'.

The Psalms were many times translated into prose and verse during the sixteenth and seventeenth centuries.[63] Such efforts were a part of the Reformation impulse that sought to place in Everyman's hands the Scriptures, which held the secrets of present and eternal life. The Psalms were turned into verse for a number of reasons. In such form, they could more easily be committed to memory. They could also be set to music and sung as a part of religious worship services and gatherings. For many years, countless thousands of Englishmen made a joyful noise unto the Lord by singing the Sternhold-Hopkins metrical versions of the Psalms which were published complete in *The Whole Book of Psalms* (1562) and included in the *Book of Common Prayer.*

In addition to translations prepared for public edification and worship, another tradition of Psalm-versification was developed by gentlemen-poets, the "courtly makers" of Tudor times. Perhaps as literary experiments, as well as acts of devotion and piety, men like Sir Thomas Wyatt and Henry Howard, Earl of Surrey, sought to bring out the "poetry" of the Psalms by deliberately artful translations. Sir Philip Sidney's was the most elaborate attempt of this sort. Bringing to his work a knowledge of other translations and of various commentaries, Sidney translated forty-three of them, employing a great variety of stanzaic and metrical patterns. Several years after his death, his sister, the Countess of Pembroke, translated the remainder; copies of the complete translation circulated in manuscript.[64]

Sidney's prestigious example; the growing body of arresting and artistic religious poetry by men like Donne, George Herbert, and Richard Crashaw; and the increasing preoccupation of individuals with their personal religious life contributed to a great vogue for translating the Psalms into verse, a vogue which developed during the seventeenth century.[65] A considerable number of these translations got into print; still others have been preserved in manuscript collections. Among the prominent figures who attempted such work are Sir John Harington, King James, Francis Bacon, Thomas Carew, Joseph Hall, John Denham, George Herbert, Henry King, Jeremy Taylor, John Milton, Sir Edwin Sandys, George Wither, and George Sandys. Davies' metaphrases were, therefore, like much of his other poetry, deeply rooted in the culture of the period of their composition.

Little is known and very little has been written about these translations.[66] What sources Davies drew upon or what commentaries he consulted are matters of conjecture. The Psalms, of course, were familiar to him from his childhood in one or more of the translations. He seems to have based his translations principally on the King James' Authorized Version, adopting occasionally a wording or figure from the Psalter appended to the *Book of Common Prayer*. In contrast to the variety in the Sidneian Psalms, Davies uniformly employs the heroic couplet; and he remains, usually, as close to the text as the demands of the couplet and the given passage permit. Grosart, who found "rare merits" in Davies' Psalms, praised them as "strikingly faithfull to the Original, and not paraphrastic."[67] Something of his close adherence to his source can be seen in the following two examples from Psalm 14.2-3:

verse 2: KING JAMES: The Lord looked down from heaven upon the children of men, to see if there were any that did understand and seek God.

DAVIES: God cast His eyes from Heauen on all mankinde,
And lookt if Hee one righteous man could finde.

verse 3:   KING JAMES: They were all gone aside, they are all to-
                            gether become filthy: there is none that
                            doeth good, no, not one.

            DAVIES: But all were wicked, all from God were
                            gone,
                            Not one did good, in all the world, not
                            one.

While Davies usually attempts to turn one verse of text into
one couplet, occasionally the spirit of the Psalm moves him to
elaborate somewhat—at times with vivid effect. For example,
the seven verses of Psalm 14 are translated into fourteen couplets
of which lines 2 and 9-16 are Davies' addition:

Psalm XIV

"There is noe God," the Foole sayth in his heart,
Yet dares not with his tongue his thought impart;
All are corrupt and odious in God's sight,
Not one doth good, not one doth well, vpright.
God cast His eyes from Heauen on all mankinde,   [5]
And lookt if Hee one righteous man could finde;
But all were wicked, all from God were gone,
Not one did good, in all the world, not one;
Their throat an open graue, their flattering tongue
And lyinge lips, like stinge of wasps haue stung.   [10]
With bitter cursing, they their mouthes doe fill;
Their feet are swift the guiltles blood to spill;
Sad, wretched mischeife, in their wayes doth lye
But for the wayes of peace they passe them by;
Noe feare of God haue they before their eyes,   [15]
Nor knowledge, while these mischeifes they deuise;
While they God's people doe with might oppresse
And eat them up like bread with greedines;
And since on God they neuer vse to call,
They fear'd when cause of feare was non at all.   [20]
But to the righteous man and to his race,
God present is with His protectinge grace;
Though fooles doe mocke the counsell of the poore,
Because in God hee trusted euermore.
Who shall saluation out of Sion giue   [25]
To Israell but God? Who shall releiue
His people and of Captiues make them free:
Thou Jacob joyfull, Israell glad shall bee.[68]

The King James' translation has so indelibly stamped itself on our consciousness that any departure from it somehow seems "wrong"; but, excepting for an occasional dissonant inversion required by meter or rhyme, Davies' translation reads very smoothly and pleasantly. As in his earlier poetry, the language is clear and graceful. The line is the basic unit of thought and most often is end-stopped, but the occasional run-on lines and the variation of the pauses within lines avoid monotony. His skillful control of the couplet is reflected in its very unobtrusiveness, and his poetry worthily anticipates the work of Waller, Denham, and Dryden.

Death came suddenly and unexpectedly to Davies in 1626, just before he was to assume the high office of Chief Justice. Although evidence for dating the composition of these translations is slight, they would seem to come late in Davies' life. It would, no doubt, have seemed appropriate to this sturdy servant of king, country, and church if he had tuned his spirit with the numbers of these Psalms shortly before taking his place in that choir of the faithful, evermore to sing his God's praises in heaven.

Conclusion

SIR John Davies probably regarded his successful career in law and government as his best piece of poetry—an artful shaping of talents, energies, and opportunities toward significant and desirable goals. The son of socially undistinguished parents, he managed to win the approbation of his social superiors, among them Queen Elizabeth and King James; to amass a considerable fortune; to see his daughter, Lucy, marry into nobility and become the Countess of Huntingdon; and to climax his career by being named Lord Chief Justice.

Although writing poetry was clearly not the principal interest of his life and was, without apparent distress, put aside as the demands of his career increased, Davies took his poetry seriously. Unlike other gentlemen-poets of his time, he saw to it that much of his work was published, and republished. No doubt he took pleasure in the popular reception which it received. His poetry repays serious consideration by students of English literature today, not only for its intrinsic literary merit and interest but also for the articulate and pleasing voice it gives to a great cultural age. His poetry embodies attitudes, assumptions, and points of view which reflect important concerns of late sixteenth-century England.

As we have seen, the *Epigrams* herald the emergence of a critical attitude toward social conduct and a realistic, almost colloquial style; *Orchestra,* if in a playful and jocular way, reflects cherished ideas of world order, harmony, and concord; and *Nosce Teipsum* voices the urgent assertions of an age seeking to retain an intellectually responsible faith amid growing doubts and challenges. Perhaps even more reflective of his age, if less explicit, is the pervasive mood of undisturbed confidence in which Davies, in whatever poetic persona, views the world and himself.

Underlying a variety of forms and tones in his poetry is an

140

easy acceptance of what is. Davies' poetry is not introspective or probing, nor does it seriously question. There is little suggestion of the individual distressingly or fearfully at odds with himself or with life which gives such compelling dramatic tension to the plays of Marlowe or to the religious poetry of Donne. Rather, Davies' poetry is unified by a sensibility of confident assertiveness: whether he is recording the inanities of a London gull, noting images of world order in the dance of life, or proclaiming the existence of God and the immortality of the human soul, his sentences are predominantly in the declarative mood. Perhaps this attitude of a serene and tranquil observer of a life devoid of mysteries most clearly demarks his poetry from that of some of his successors in the earlier part of the seventeenth century.

Davies was also, as George Saintsbury described him, "a versesmith."[69] At a time when English poetry was experimenting with prosody and style—was in effect still seeking its own voice and language—Davies demonstrated a felicitous command of exacting verse forms like the sonnet, rhyme-royal stanza, quatrain, and heroic couplet and a flexibility in making these forms convey a pleasing variety of tones. In addition, he perfected a medium of language which was plain and conversational, avoided extravagance either in figure or vocabulary, and, at its best, achieved an aesthetically pleasing lucidity. The perfection of such "classic" qualities by Davies, as well as others like Samuel Daniel and Ben Jonson, would in later times serve as a norm from which poets might for a time depart in exciting and striking stylistic ways but to which English poetry would return, to the refreshment of its readers and to the renewal of its linguistic energies.

Among an impressive choir of English Renaissance singers, Davies sang his small part artfully; and he did so in a voice whose music later poets such as Pope, Johnson, Wordsworth, Coleridge, Eliot, and Roethke have enjoyed and heard with profit.[70]

Notes and References

Chapter One

1. For biographical information, I am principally indebted to A. B. Grosart's Memorial-Introduction to *The Complete Works of Sir John Davies* (Blackburn, 1869–1876), supplemented by the unpublished B. Litt. thesis at the Bodleian Library of T. J. Childs, "An Edition of *Nosce Teipsum* by Sir John Davies," 1939, and Bodleian MS. Carte 62, ff. 590–1: "Notes of the Life of Sr John Dauys," dated May 2, 1674. For a discussion of the Carte "Notes" and their likely relationship to similar biographical notes among the Hastings Papers now at the Henry E. Huntington Library (where they are identified as "Genealogical HA L5A5"), see the able work of J. R. Brink, "The Composition Date of Sir John Davies' *Nosce Teipsum*," *Huntington Library Quarterly*, XXXVI (1973): 28–32. I am indebted to Dr. Robert Krueger for calling the Hastings Genealogical Papers to my attention and providing me with some information concerning them.

2. For a genealogy see Richard C. Hoare, *The History of Modern Wiltshire* (London, 1822–1844), IV: 136. The Carte "Notes" as do the Hastings give Edward as the poet's father's name. Brink, *op. cit.*, p. 25, n. 19, insists that Edward is the correct name. As noted later, however, the record of Davies' admission to the Middle Temple names him as the son of John.

3. John Aubrey's letter to Elias Ashmole, Bodleian MS. Autog. d. 21, f. 147; Anthony à Wood, *Athenae Oxonienses and Fasti Oxonienses*, ed. Philip Bliss (London, 1813–1820), II: 400.

4. Grosart, Memorial-Introduction, pp. xxi–xxii.

5. Thomas F. Kirby, *Winchester Scholars* (London, 1888), p. 149.

6. A. F. Leach, *Educational Charters and Documents 598 to 1909* (Cambridge, 1911), p. 321.

7. For the curriculum at Winchester College, see T. W. Baldwin, *William Shakespeare's Small Latine & Lesse Greek* (Urbana, 1944), I: 321 ff.

8. I have drawn on Craig R. Thompson, "Schools in Tudor England," in *Life and Letters in Tudor and Stuart England*, ed. Louis B. Wright and Virginia A. LaMar (Ithaca, 1958): 285–334, and M. H. Curtis, "Education and Apprenticeship," *Shakespeare Survey*, XVII (1964): 53–72.

9. *Register of the University of Oxford*, ed. Andrew Clark (Oxford, 1889), II, pt. ii: 147.

10. Craig R. Thompson, "Universities in Tudor England," in *Life and Letters*, ed. Wright and LaMar, pp. 335–82.

11. Wood, *Athenae Oxon.*, II: 400.

12. Joseph Foster, *Alumni Oxonienses*, 1500–1714 (Oxford, 1891–1892), p. 328.

13. Wood, *Fasti Oxon.*, V: 250.

14. *Register*, ed. Clark, II, pt. III: 160.

15. Joan Simon, *Education and Society in Tudor England* (Cambridge, 1966), pp. 356–58.

16. *Middle Temple Records*, ed. Charles H. Hopwood (London, 1904–1905), I: 296.

17. J. Bruce Williamson, *The History of the Temple* (London, 1924), p. 214.

18. *A Survey of London*, ed. Charles L. Kingsford (Oxford, 1908), I: 78.

19. Quoted in Simon, *Education and Society*, p. 355.

20. For information on the life and study at the Inns, I am indebted to Williamson, *History of the Temple*, and Robert Ingpen, *Six Lectures on the Inns of Court and Chancery* (London, 1912).

21. Kenneth Charlton, "Liberal Education and the Inns of Court in the Sixteenth Century," *British Journal of Educational Studies*, IX (1960–61): 37.

22. Quoted from G. M. Young by A. L. Rowse, *The England of Elizabeth* (New York, 1961), p. 523.

23. See Philip J. Finkelpearl, *John Marston of the Middle Temple* (Cambridge, U.S.A., 1969), Chapters V–VI, for information on the masques and revels.

24. See T. F. Reddaway, "London and the Court," *Shakespeare Survey*, XVII (1964): 3–12.

25. *Middle Temple Records*, ed. Hopwood, I: 318.

26. *Ibid.*, 326–27.

27. Childs, pp. 14–23. The letters are Bodleian MS. D'Orville 52, ff. 49–50.

28. Childs, p. 17; Merula's letter is in Brit. Museum MS. Cotton Julius, C.v.f. 49 (*olim* 44).

29. Translation by Childs, pp. 16–18, n. 1.

30. Wood, *Athenae Oxon.*, II: 402.

31. Sig. Q3^v, cited by Childs, p. 30.

32. *Middle Temple Records*, ed. Hopwood, I: 354.

33. *Ibid.*, 379–80. Pertinent information concerning this cele-

brated event was collected by Lord Stowell in *Archaeologia*, XXI (1826): 107–12.

34. I am indebted to the article on Martin in the *Dictionary of National Biography* for this biographical information.

35. *Brief Lives*, ed. Andrew Clark (Oxford, 1898), II: 48–49.

36. *Archaeologia*, p. 109, n. a.

37. Wood, *Athenae Oxon.*, II: 400.

38. George Chalmers, ed., *Historical Tracts* (London, 1786), p. iii.

39. "Sir John Davies and the 'Prince d'Amour'," *Notes and Queries*, X (1963): 300–2.

40. Bodleian MS. Rawl. Poet. 148, f. 4^r.

41. Humphrey W. Woolrych, *Lives of Eminent Serjeants-at-Law of the English Bar* (London, 1869), I: 190.

42. Wood, *Athenae Oxon.*, II: 401.

43. These are printed by Thomas Hearne, *A Collection of Curious Discourses Written by Eminent Antiquarians upon Several Heads in Our English Antiquities* (London, 1771).

44. Childs seems to have been the first to note this unpublished paper which is preserved in Brit. Mus. MS. Cotton Faustina E.V. ff. 168–71, in Davies' handwriting.

45. I draw biographical information on these figures from the *Dictionary of National Biography*.

46. W. W. Greg, *English Literary Autographs 1550–1650* (London, 1925–1932), II, plate XLVII.

47. Brit. Mus. MS. Lansdowne, 88, art. 17, f. 34^r, cited by Childs, p. 47.

48. See Virgil B. Heltzel, "Sir Thomas Egerton as Patron," *Huntington Library Quarterly*, XI (1948): 105–27.

49. *The Complete Poems of Sir John Davies*, ed. A. B. Grosart (London, 1876), II: 112–13.

50. *Works*, ed. Grosart, II: 284.

51. Wood, *Athenae Oxon.*, II: 401.

52. Huntington Lib. MS. HA 2522.

53. *The Letters of John Chamberlain*, ed. Norman E. McClure (Philadelphia, 1939), I: 126.

54. Quoted by Lord Stowell, p. 111. See note 33.

55. *Ibid.*, p. 112.

56. *Letters*, ed. McClure, I: 189.

57. Quoted by Woolrych, p. 196.

58. Wood, *Athenae Oxon.*, II: 401. J. R. Brink, *op. cit.*, p. 21, argues that this anecdote relates to 1594, when Davies was first introduced to James in Scotland.

59. *Letters*, ed. McClure, I: 192.

60. Grosart, Memorial-Introduction, p. xli.

61. For this brief account of Davies' work in Ireland, I am indebted to Vol. I of S. R. Gardiner's *History of England from the Accession of James I to the Outbreak of the Civil War. 1603–1642* (London, 1900), Richard Bagwell, *Ireland Under the Stuarts* (London, 1909), and C. Litton Falkiner, "Sir John Davies," *Essays Relating to Ireland* (London, 1909), pp. 32–55.

62. See George Chalmers, *Historical Tracts: by Sir John Davies, Attorney General* (London, 1786), and Grosart, Memorial-Introduction, pp. xlvi ff.

63. *Historical MSS Commission Report. The Manuscripts of the Late Reginald Rawdon Hastings, Esq.*, ed. Francis Bickley (London, 1947), IV: 2–3.

64. For the address, see Chalmers, pp. 295–317.

65. *Calendar of the State Papers, relating to Ireland, of the Reign of James I. 1611–1614*, ed. C. W. Russell and John P. Prendergast (London, 1877), pp. 517–18.

66. George Hill, *An Historical Account of the Plantation of Ulster, 1608–1620* (Belfast, 1877), pp. 245, 271, 330, 485, 537, and 569.

67. *Letters*, ed. McClure, I: 288.

68. George Ballard, *Memoirs of Several Ladies of Great Britain* (Oxford, 1752), pp. 271–80.

69. Wood, *Athenae Oxon.*, II: 404.

70. Reprinted by Grosart, *Works*, II: 1–168. A facsimile of the 1612 edition, ed. John Barry, has been published by the Irish University Press (Shannon, 1969).

71. *Ibid.*, III: 249–87.

72. *Ibid.*, 284.

73. *Ibid.*, 169–242. Concerning the attribution of this work to Davies see Grosart's Memorial-Introduction, pp. cxcv–cxcvi.

74. *Dictionary of National Biography.*

75. See Theodore Spencer, "The History of an Unfortunate Lady," *Harvard Studies and Notes in Philology and Literature*, XX (1938): 43–59, for the curious and pathetic details.

76. Wood, *Athenae Oxon.*, II: 403.

77. Huntington Library MS. HA 1930.

78. Wood, *Athenae Oxon.*, II: 403. I have seen no suggestion that Davies' sudden death was from other than natural causes, but Eleanor's instability and determined allegiance to her mission, her dispute with her unsympathetic husband, and the remarkable accuracy of her prognostication concerning his death add a certain intriguing resonance to Wood's casual statement that Davies was "found dead in his bed, by an apoplexy, *as 'twas said.*" (italics mine),

and cause one to wonder whether Davies' death might have been aided by a self-serving prophetess.

79. *Ibid.*, 404.

Chapter Two

1. On the literary satire in this decade see Alvin Kernan, *The Cankered Muse: Satire in the English Renaissance* (New Haven, 1959), Anthony Caputi, *John Marston, Satirist* (Ithaca, 1961), and Bernard Harris, "Dissent and Satire," *Shakespeare Survey*, XVII (1964): 120–37.

2. Quoted by C. H. Herford and Percy Simpson, eds., *Ben Jonson* (Oxford, 1925–1952), I: 11.

3. A brief summary of these views can be found in John Wilcox, "Informal Publication of Late Sixteenth Century Verse Satire," *Huntington Library Quarterly*, XIII (1950): 191–200.

4. For a study of these early editions, see Tucker Brooke, "The Marlowe Canon," *PMLA*, XXXVII (1922): 367–417.

5. *A Transcript of the Stationers' Registers*, ed. Edward Arber (London, 1875), III: 678.

6. "The Publication of Marlowe's 'Elegies' and Davies' 'Epigrams'," *Review of English Studies*, IV (1953): 260–61.

7. Elizabeth Donno has challenged Nosworthy's date in her edition of Harington's *The Metamorphosis of Ajax* (London, 1962), p. 103.

8. J. William Hebel and Hoyt H. Hudson, eds., *Poetry of the English Renaissance* (New York, 1929), p. 966.

9. Wilcox, "Informal Publication," p. 197, n. 13.

10. J. M. Nosworthy, "Marlowe's *Ovid* and Davies' *Epigrams*— A Postscript," *Review of English Studies*, XV (1964): 397–98.

11. Quoted by Bernard Harris, "Men like Satyrs," in *Elizabethan Poetry*, ed. J. R. Brown and Bernard Harris, Stratford-Upon-Avon Studies, no. 2 (London, 1960), p. 181.

12. Hoyt H. Hudson, *The Epigram in the English Renaissance* (Princeton, 1947), pp. 145–69.

13. The principal manuscript collections of Davies' *Epigrams* are Bodleian MS. Rawlinson Poetry 212, Bodleian MS. Add. 97, British Museum Harleian MS. 1836, Rosenbach Museum MS. 1083/15, and Cambridge University Library MS. Kk.1.3.

14. A good sampling of the epigram of this period can be found in *Poetry of the English Renaissance*, ed. Hebel and Hudson, pp. 520–34.

15. *Ben Jonson*, VIII: 1–89.

16. *Ibid.*, 27.

17. *Quodlibets* (1628), p. 15.

18. *Skialetheia* (1598), Shakespeare Association Facsimiles, No. 2 (London, 1931), Epigram 20.

19. Ed. J. B. Leishman (London, 1949), p. 240.

20. Ed. Norman E. McClure (Philadelphia, 1930), p. 306.

21. For these and other parallels see T. K. Whipple, *Martial and the English Epigram* (Berkeley, 1925), pp. 338–40. The translation of Martial (II,xvi) is by W. C. Ker, *Martial* (New York, 1919), I: 119–21.

22. For texts of epigrams recently attributed to Davies, see Robert Krueger, "Sir John Davies: *Orchestra* Complete, *Epigrams*, Unpublished Poems," *Review of English Studies*, XIII (1962): 123–24. Dr. Krueger informs me that in his forthcoming edition of Davies' poetry he will propose additional attributions to Davies' canon. Most of these attributions are bawdy epigrams. Several of them attack Sir Edward Coke and Bishop Richard Fletcher.

23. Texts of the *Epigrams* are cited from *The Complete Poems of Sir John Davies*, ed. A. B. Grosart (London, 1876), II: 7–47.

24. Herford and Simpson, eds., *Ben Jonson*, II: 346.

25. For a delightful extended satire on the gull, see Thomas Dekker's *The Guls Horne-booke* (1609).

26. "Two Classic Elizabethans: Samuel Daniel and Sir John Davies" in *Theodore Spencer: Selected Essays*, ed. Alan C. Purves (New Brunswick, 1966), p. 116.

27. The two texts are reprinted from Percy Simpson "Unpublished Epigrams of Sir John Davies," *Review of English Studies*, III (1952): 50.

28. *Ben Jonson*, I: 137.

29. Clare Howard, ed., *The Poems of Sir John Davies* (New York, 1941), p. 248.

30. J. H. Penniman, *War of the Theatres* (Boston, 1897), p. 109; C. J. Bishop, "Raleigh Satirized by Harington and Davies," *Review of English Studies*, XXIII (1972): 52–56.

31. Howard reprints these poems in *Poems of Sir John Davies*, pp. 59–60.

32. The only known early text of these sonnets appears in the Dr. Farmer Chetham MS. in the Chetham Library, Manchester. A. B. Grosart edited this MS. in two volumes for the Chetham Society in 1873, and reprinted the *Gulling Sonnets* in the 1876 edition of Davies' poems (II: 53–62).

33. Hallett Smith, *Elizabethan Poetry: A Study in Conventions, Meaning, and Expression* (Cambridge, U.S.A., 1952), pp. 132–35.

34. *Ibid.*, p. 142.

35. The Elizabethan sonnet has received much scholarly attention. In addition to Smith, *Elizabethan Poetry*, pp. 131–93, see Lisle C. John, *The Elizabethan Sonnet Sequences* (New York, 1938).

36. Sidney Lee, "The Elizabethan Sonnet," in *Cambridge History of English Literature*, ed. A. W. Ward *et al.* (New York, 1907–1933), III: 385.

37. Arnold Davenport, ed., *The Collected Poems of Joseph Hall* (Liverpool, 1949), p. xxxvi. See particularly Satires I, i and vii; IV, ii, and VI, i.

38. An excellent brief consideration of these patterns of writing can be found in Hudson, *The Epigram in the English Renaissance*, pp. 156–69.

39. Hudson (*ibid.*, p. 164 and p. 165, n. 31) cites Spenser's *Faerie Queene*, II, iv, 35, and Milton's *Paradise Lost*, II, 947–49.

40. Hyder E. Rollins, ed. (Cambridge, U.S.A., 1931), pp. 79–80, 173–78.

41. P. Burwell Rogers, "Sir John Davies' *Gulling Sonnets*," *Bucknell University Studies*, IV (1954): 193.

42. *Zepheria* (1594). Printed for the Spenser Society (Manchester, 1869), p. 24.

43. *Poems*, ed. Grosart, II: 217–22, 225, 227–28, 239–40.

44. *A Poetical Rhapsody*, ed. Hyder E. Rollins (Cambridge, U.S.A., 1931), I: 203–12; for Rollins' useful notes, see II: 176–79.

45. *Poems*, ed. Grosart, II: 99–106. Texts of the *Sonnets*, however, are quoted from Rollins' edition of the *Rhapsody*.

46. *Poems*, ed. Grosart, I: cix–cx.

Chapter Three

1. *Stationers' Registers*, ed. Arber, II: 665.

2. Citations of *Orchestra* are to the edition of E. M. W. Tillyard (London, 1945).

3. *Epigrams of Sir John Harington*, ed. McClure, pp. 211–12.

4. *The Works of Thomas Nashe*, ed. R. B. McKerrow (London, 1904–1910), III: 177.

5. *The Works of John Marston*, ed. A. H. Bullen (London, 1877), III: 372.

6. A. H. Bullen, ed., *Some Longer Elizabethan Poems* (Westminster, 1903), p. vii.

7. Margarete Seemann, *Sir John Davies, sein Leben und seine Werke* (Vienna, 1913), pp. 52–54.

8. Herbert Howarth, *The Tiger's Heart* (New York, 1970), p. 182.

9. Martin is the "swallow" of St. 131 (See E. K. Chambers' notes in *The Oxford Book of Sixteenth Century Verse* [Oxford, 1932], pp. 884–85).

10. Tillyard, ed., *Orchestra*, p. 115.

11. Krueger, "Sir John Davies," pp. 20–29.

12. *Ibid.*, pp. 20–24.

13. *Ibid.*, p. 26.

14. E. M. W. Tillyard, *Five Poems, 1470–1870* (London, 1948), pp. 30–48.

15. Muriel C. Bradbrook, *Shakespeare and Elizabethan Poetry* (London, 1951), p. 66. G. A. Wilkes has also noted the relationship of *Orchestra* to the mythological poem, "The poetry of Sir John Davies," *Huntington Library Quarterly*, XXV (1962): 283–98.

16. For a discussion of the mythological poem, see Hallett Smith, *Elizabethan Poetry* (Cambridge, U.S.A., 1953), pp. 64–130.

17. David Daiches, *A Critical History of English Literature* (London, 1960), I: 348–49.

18. Concerning the revels at Gray's Inn in 1594–95, see *Gesta Grayorum 1688*, ed. W. W. Greg, Malone Society Reprint (Oxford, 1914); for those at the Middle Temple in 1597–98, see Benjamin Rudyard's *Le Prince d'Amour or the Prince of Love* (1660).

19. Finkelpearl, *John Marston*, p. 78.

20. *Ibid.*, p. 77. Additional support for the notion that *Orchestra* was recited is offered by T. W. Craik, "Volpone's Young Antinous," *Notes and Queries*, XVII (1970): 213–14.

21. Northrop Frye, *Anatomy of Criticism* (New York, 1968), p. 310. David Hadas, unpubl. doctoral diss. (Columbia, 1963), "The Mind and Art of Sir John Davies," p. 125, less appropriately, in my judgment, relates the poem to Frye's "symposium" (*Anatomy*, pp. 286 ff.).

22. Frye, *ibid.*, p. 311.

23. *Idem.*

24. Louise Brown Osborne, *The Life, Letters, and Writings of John Hoskyns 1566–1638* (New Haven, 1937), p. 136.

25. Tillyard, *Five Poems*, p. 33.

26. *The Dialogues of Plato*, trans. Benjamin Jowett (New York, 1937), II: 21–22.

27. Quoted in Curt Sachs, *World History of the Dance*, trans. Bessie Schonberg (New York, 1937), p. 124.

28. *The Essays and Hymns of Synesios of Cyrene*, trans. Augustus Fitzgerald (London, 1930), II: 374.

29. *Ibid.*, 385. I am indebted to A. C. Patrides for calling these passages to my attention.

30. *The Complete Works of Joshua Sylvester,* ed. A. B. Grosart (London, 1880), I: 84, and I: 157; *Selected Essays of Montaigne,* trans. John Florio, ed. Walter Kaiser (Boston, 1964), p. 216; and Nan C. Carpenter, "The Place of Music in 'L'Allegro' and 'Il Penseroso'," *University of Toronto Quarterly,* XXII (1953): 354–67.

31. Frances A. Yates, *The French Academies of the Sixteenth Century* (London, 1947).

32. John C. Meagher, "The Dance and the Masques of Ben Jonson," *Journal of the Warburg and Courtauld Institutes,* XXV (1962): 258–77.

33. J. R. Brown, *Shakespeare and His Comedies* (London, 1957), pp. 139–59.

34. A. H. Bullen, *Some Longer Poems,* pp. viii-xi.

35. Lucian, *Peri Orkheseos,* trans. A.M. Harmon, Loeb Classical Library (Cambridge, U.S.A., 1936), V: 221.

36. *Ibid.,* 231.

37. *Ibid.,* 232–33.

38. Tillyard, *Five Poems,* pp. 36–37.

39. Sir Thomas Eylot, *The Boke Named the Gouernour,* ed. Henry H. S. Croft (London, 1883), I, chs. xix–xxv. Concerning Elyot's treatment of dancing see John M. Major, "The Moralization of the Dance in Elyot's *Governour,*" *Studies in the Renaissance,* V (1958): 26–36.

40. Little has been written about La Tour. Biographical information and brief notices of his poems can be found in Henry Vaschalde, "La Poète Bérenger de la Tour et ses Oeuvres," *Revue du Lyonnais,* XII (1891): 46–60, 99–116, 173–90, 228–47. For a more extended discussion of Davies and La Tour see my essay "Bérenger de La Tour and Sir John Davies: Two Poets Who Set the Planets Dancing," *The Library Chronicle,* XXXVII (1971): 116–25.

41. Tillyard, *Five Poems,* pp. 43–47.

42. See Rosamond Tuve, "A Medieval Commonplace in Spenser's Cosmology," *Studies in Philology,* XXX (1933): 133.

43. David Hadas, too, has noted the relevance of this debate to *Orchestra* (diss., p. 12); for studies of the controversy, see Charles R. Baskervill, *The Elizabethan Jig* (Chicago, 1929), pp. 335–69, and H. P. Clive, "The Calvinists and the Question of Dancing in the 16th Century," *Bibliothèque d'Humanisme,* XXIII (1961): 296–323.

44. Philip Stubbes, *Anatomy of Abuses,* ed. Frederick J. Furnivall (London, 1877–1879), Pt. I, pp. 154, 155–56.

45. Author of *Orchesographie* (Langres, 1588), a treatise in dialogue form defending dancing and instructing the reader in the execution of various dances.

46. See his *Positions* (1581), ed. Robert H. Quick (London, 1888), ch. 16: "On Daunsing, why it is blamed, and how deliuered from blame," pp. 72–75.

47. See Elkin C. Wilson, *England's Eliza* (Cambridge, U.S.A., 1939), pp. 260–61.

48. Alexander Chalmers, ed., *The Works of the English Poets from Chaucer to Cowper* (London, 1810), V: 78.

49. C. S. Lewis, *English Literature in the Sixteenth Century* (Oxford, 1954), p. 526.

50. See, for example, Hardin Craig, *The Enchanted Glass* (New York, 1935), Arthur O. Lovejoy, *The Great Chain of Being* (New York, 1936), Theodore Spencer, *Shakespeare and the Nature of Man* (New York, 1942), and C. S. Lewis, *The Discarded Image* (Cambridge, 1964).

51. As an instance, see Herbert Howarth's chapter entitled "Put Away the World-Picture," in *The Tiger's Heart*, pp. 165–91.

52. E. M. W. Tillyard, *The Elizabethan World Picture* (London, 1943).

53. A. C. Patrides, "The Numerological Approach to Cosmic Order during the English Renaissance," *Isis*, LXIX (1958): 391–97.

54. Davies, *Poems*, ed. Grosart, II: 96–98.

55. Tillyard, ed., *Orchestra*, p. 10.

56. Tillyard, *Elizabethan World Picture*, pp. 94–99.

57. G. A. Wilkes, "The Poetry of Sir John Davies," pp. 288–89.

58. *Ibid.*, pp. 289–90.

59. The echo of this stanza by Coleridge in *The Rhyme of the Ancient Mariner* has been noted by several; see Frederick E. Pierce, "Coleridge and Sir John Davies," *Modern Language Notes*, XLV (1930): 395.

60. Lewis, *English Literature in the Sixteenth Century*, p. 4.

Chapter Four

1. See, for example, Phoebe Sheavyn, *The Literary Profession in the Elizabethan Age* (Manchester, 1909), and John F. Danby, *Poets on Fortune's Hill* (London, 1952).

2. Danby, pp. 15 ff.

3. *Ibid.*, p. 36.

4. *Ibid.*, p. 37.

5. *Poems*, ed. Grosart, I: 9–10.

6. *Ibid.*, 11.

7. Childs, p. 42.

8. Grosart reprints the Northumberland dedication in his edition of the *Poems*, I: 12–13.

9. *Ibid.*, II: 222–23.

10. Robert Krueger, unpubl. diss. (Oxford, 1965), "A Critical Edition of the Poems of Sir John Davies," pp. 690 and 654. For texts see *Poems*, ed. Grosart, II: 213–14 and 227–28.

11. *Poems*, ed. Grosart, I: 125–54.

12. John M. Robertson, *Elizabethan Literature* (New York, 1914), p. 151.

13. Lewis, *English Literature in the Sixteenth Century*, p. 526.

14. Concerning poetry of such formal patterns see the brief article "Elizabethan Decoration: Patterns in Art and Passion," *Times Literary Supplement*, July 3, 1937, pp. 485–96, and Margaret Church, "The First English Pattern Poems," *PMLA*, LXI (1946): 630–50.

15. A. Kent Hieatt, *Short Time's Endless Monument* (New York, 1960).

16. Bradbrook, *Shakespeare and Elizabethan Poetry*, pp. 18 ff.

17. For my discussion of Astraea, I draw on Frances Yates, "Elizabeth as Astraea," *Journal of the Warburg and Courtauld Institutes* X (1947): 27–82.

18. *Ibid.*, p. 30.

19. *Ibid.*, pp. 35–37.

20. Concerning Astraea's apparently paradoxical association with both spring and autumn, see Miss Yates, "Elizabeth as Astraea," pp. 64–65.

21. Grosart prints one of these (*Poems*, II: 107).

22. *Ibid.*, 112–13.

23. Quoted by Grosart, ed., *Works*, I: 303–4.

24. *Poems*, ed. Grosart, II: 229–36.

25. *Ibid.*, 230–31.

26. See David H. Wilson, *King James VI and I* (London, 1956), pp. 168–74, concerning the praise heaped upon the king.

27. *Poems*, ed. Grosart, II: 238–39.

28. *Ibid.*, 223–25.

29. Falconer Madan, *A Summary Catalogue of Western Manuscripts in the Bodleian Library* (Oxford, 1895–1953), Entry no. 29419.

30. Childs, pp. 188 ff.

31. Robert Krueger, "Sir John Davies," pp. 113–18.

32. *Ibid.*, p. 113.

33. I have collated my transcription with Krueger's and adopted one or two of his emendations. I have silently expanded scribal abbreviations and followed modern typological conventions.

34. *Poems*, ed. Grosart, II: 38–39.

35. Childs, p. 188; Krueger, "Sir John Davies," p. 113. For additional, anonymous verses written for this wedding, see my note,

"Three Unpublished Elizabethan Wedding Poems," *Modern Language Review*, LVIII (1963): 217–19.

36. For the brief historical review of the epithalamion, I am indebted to the excellent work of Virginia Tufte's unpubl. doctoral diss. (University of California at Los Angeles, 1964), "Literary Backgrounds and Motifs of the Epithalamium in English to 1650." Unfortunately, Miss Tufte overlooked Davies' poem.

37. Sir Philip Sidney, *The Poems of Sir Philip Sidney*, ed. William A. Ringler (Oxford, 1962), pp. 91–94.

38. *The Works of Edmund Spenser: A Variorum Edition*, ed. Edwin Greenlaw *et al.*, VII (Baltimore, 1947): 323.

39. Virginia Tufte, "Literary Background of the Epithalamium," p. 172. For Baïf's poem see *Euvres en Rime de Ian Antoine de Baïf*, ed. Ch. Martz-Laveaux (Paris, 1883), II: 352–58.

40. For a discussion of the thematic conventions of the epithalamion see Thomas M. Greene, "Spenser and the Epithalamic Convention," *Comparative Literature*, IX (1957): 215–28. The dramatic potential of Davies' poem has also been noted by J. R. Brink, "The Masque of the Nine Muses: Sir John Davies's Unpublished 'Epithalamion' and the 'Belphoebe-Ruby' Episode in *The Faerie Queene*," *Review of English Studies*, XXIII (1972): 445–47, who offers some convincing contemporary evidence that it was presented as a pageant at the wedding of Elizabeth Vere and William Stanley.

41. Hyder E. Rollins, ed., *A Poetical Rhapsody* (Cambridge, U.S.A., 1931), I: 239–55.

42. *Poems*, ed. Grosart, II: 65–71.

43. *Ibid.*, I: cxviii.

44. *Ibid.*, cxviii–cxix.

45. Childs, p. 46; C. Howard, ed., p. vi; Krueger, diss., p. xxxiii.

46. I am indebted to Robert Krueger (diss., p. 682) for calling my attention to this exhibit.

47. Rollins, ed., *A Poetical Rhapsody*, II: 199.

48. J. E. Neale, *Queen Elizabeth* (London, 1934), pp. 205–19.

49. *Ibid.*, p. 209.

50. *Ibid.*, pp. 209–10.

51. Chamberlain, *Letters*, I: 160.

52. Rollins, ed., I: 246. See Rollins' excellent notes, II: 202–10.

53. *Poems*, ed. Grosart, II: 87–95. An account of the *Lottery* is given in John Ashton, *A History of Lotteries* (New York, 1893), pp. 24–27.

54. Grosart, ed. *Poems*, I: cxi–cxii.

55. A text of this song set to music is in Robert Jones, *Ultimum Vale* (1608).

56. In three manuscripts cited by Rollins (*Poetical Rhapsody*, II: 202–8), which preserve texts of the lots, the drawers' names are indicated, possibly confirming Robert Krueger's suggestion that the lots were not really drawn by chance and that Davies had devised them in most instances specifically for individual recipients (diss., p. 665).

57. John Nichols, *The Progresses of Queen Elizabeth* (London, 1823), III: 586–95. For a succinct account of the Harefield Entertainment, see E. K. Chambers, *Elizabethan Stage*, IV: 67–68.

58. *Poems*, ed. Grosart, II: 243–58.

59. *Ibid.*, I: cxvi.

60. Nichols, III: 595, n. 2.

61. Grosart, ed. *Poems*, I: cxiii.

62. *Idem.*

63. Chambers, *Elizabethan Stage*, IV: 68.

64. Chamberlain, *Letters*, I: 176.

65. *Diary of John Manningham*, ed. John Bruce, Camden Society Publication 99 (London, 1898), pp. 99–100.

66. Chamberlain, *Letters*, I: 177. For the text see *Poems*, ed. Grosart, II: 72–86.

Chapter Five

1. Hebel and Hudson, eds., *Poetry of the English Renaissance*, p. 966.

2. See Louis B. Wright, *Middle-Class Culture in Elizabethan England* (Chapel Hill, 1935), Chap. VIII, "Guides to Godliness," pp. 228–96 and "The Significance of Religious Writings in the English Renaissance," *Journal of the History of Ideas*, I (1940): 59–68.

3. For studies of this material see Robert B. Thornburg, unpubl. doctoral diss. (University of Pennsylvania, 1956), "A Survey of Sixteenth-Century English Religious Verse," and Lily B. Campbell, *Divine Poetry and Drama in Sixteenth-Century England* (Berkeley, 1961).

4. Wright, *Middle-Class Culture*, p. 229.

5. Wood, *Athenae Oxon*, II: 400–401.

6. *Ibid.*, 401.

7. Ed. Arber, III: 49.

8. Grosart, ed. *Poems*, I: xxiv.

9. *Poems*, ed. Grosart, I: 23–24.

10. I am indebted in the review of evidence for the dating of *Nosce Teipsum* principally to the Reverend Childs' dissertation, pp. 40–42. A particularly interesting and important recent discussion of this topic is J. R. Brink, "The Composition Date of Sir John Davies' *Nosce Teipsum*," cited earlier in this book. To the evidence compiled by Reverend Childs, Brink adds a careful study of the manuscript evidence bearing on the poem, offers a most interesting speculation that the poem was alluded to during the student revels at the Middle Temple on December 27, 1597, and concludes that *Nosce Teipsum* "was completed in manuscript by the summer of 1594" (*ibid.*, p. 27).

11. Grosart, ed., *Poems*, I: xxvi, n. 8.

12. Fol. 590.

13. *Works*, ed. McKerrow, I: 258.

14. *Ibid.*, IV: 157. John Sparrow, "Some Later Editions of John Davies's *Nosce Teipsum*," *Library*, N.S. I (1946): 136–42, also supports this view.

15. *Poems*, ed. Grosart, I: 33–34.

16. Childs, pp. 40–42.

17. Fol. 590.

18. Wood, *Athenae Oxon.*, I: 401.

19. Wilkes, "Poetry of Sir John Davies," p. 292.

20. I am indebted for information concerning the *nosce* theme to Eliza G. Wilkins, *The Delphic Maxims in Literature* (Chicago, 1929), Chs. IV, V, and VI.

21. Quoted by Louis I. Bredvold, "The Sources Used by Davies in *Nosce Teipsum*," *PMLA*, XXXVIII (1923): 748–49, from pp. 10–12 of the English translation of Primaudaye by "T.B.," entitled *The Second Part of the French Academie* (1594).

22. For this perspective on *Nosce Teipsum* and the ensuing discussion of atheism, I am indebted to George T. Buckley, *Atheism in the English Renaissance* (Chicago, 1932). Concerning the shared traditions of *Nosce Teipsum* and Greville's *Of Human Learning* and similar poems, see R. L. Colie, "The Rhetoric of Transcendence," *Philological Quarterly*, XLIII (1964): 145–70.

23. Quoted by Buckley, p. 44.

24. *Ibid.*, pp. 63–64.

25. *Ibid.*, pp. 71–72.

26. *Ibid.*, pp. 100–103.

27. *Poems*, ed. Grosart, I: 82–83.

28. *Ibid.*, 95–110.

29. Grosart, ed., *Poems*, I: lxi.

30. *Ibid.*, lxi–lxiii.

31. E. H. Sneath, *Philosophy in Poetry* (New York, 1903), p. 47.

32. Seemann, *Sir John Davies*, pp. 24–38. A recent able discussion of sources and intellectual background is Ruby D. Nemser's unpubl. doctoral diss. (Harvard, 1965), "Introduction and Notes for an Edition of *Nosce Teipsum*."

33. Bredvold, "Sources," and George T. Buckley, "The Indebtedness of *Nosce Teipsum* to Mornay's *Trunesse of the Christian Religion*," *Modern Philology*, XXV (1927): 67–78.

34. Bredvold, "Sources," *passim*.

35. Buckley, "Indebtedness of *Nosce Teipsum*," pp. 72–78.

36. *Poems*, ed. Grosart, I: 105.

37. Quoted by Buckley, "The Indebtedness of *Nosce Teipsum*," p. 76, from *Trunesse of the Christian Religion* (1587), p. 236.

38. Buckley, *Atheism in the English Renaissance*, pp. 117–20.

39. Sneath, *Philosophy in Poetry*, provides a very detailed summary of the poem and a discussion of the background of the ideas presented.

40. *Poems*, ed. Grosart, I: 16.

41. *Ibid.*, 17.

42. Sneath, pp. 57–62.

43. *Poems*, ed. Grosart, I: 18.

44. *Ibid.*, 21.

45. *Ibid.*, 22.

46. *Ibid.*, 23.

47. *Ibid.*, 24.

48. *Ibid.*, 28–29.

49. *Ibid.*, 29–30.

50. *Ibid.*, 75.

51. *Ibid.*, 78–79.

52. *Ibid.*, 81.

53. *Ibid.*, 85.

54. Krueger, diss., p. xxxi. For comment on the later publication of *Nosce Teipsum*, see Richard H. Perkinson, "The Polemical Use of Davies' *Nosce Teipsum*," *Studies in Philology*, XXXVI (1939): 597–608, and "Additional Observations on the Later Editions of *Nosce Teipsum*," *Library*, N.S. II (1947): 61–63; and John Sparrow, "Some Later Editions of *Nosce Teipsum*," pp. 136–42.

55. Felix E. Schelling, *English Literature During the Lifetime of Shakespeare* (New York, 1910), p. 218.

56. T. S. Eliot, "Sir John Davies" in *On Poetry and Poets* (New York, 1957), pp. 149–55.

57. *Ibid.*, p. 151.

58. Spencer, "Two Classic Elizabethans," p. 111.

59. Frye, *Anatomy of Criticism*, pp. 163–70.

60. Eliot, p. 154. Although approached from a different perspective, J. R. Brink, "The Rhetorical Structure of Sir John Davies's *Nosce Teipsum*," *Yearbook of English Studies*, IV (1974): 52–61, offers a reading of the poem and its unity similar to that proposed above.

61. Wood, *Athenae Oxon.*, II: 403.

62. *Poems*, ed. Grosart, II: 119–207; for the bases of his attribution see *ibid.*, 201, n. 3.

63. For useful background comment, see Hallett Smith, "English Metrical Psalms in the Sixteenth Century and Their Literary Significance," *Huntington Library Quarterly*, IX (1946): 249–71; and Campbell, *Divine Poetry and Drama*, pp. 34–54.

64. For the complete translation, see *The Psalms of Sir Philip Sidney and the Countess of Pembroke*, ed. J. C. A. Rathmell (New York, 1963), which contains a useful introduction.

65. See Philipp von Rohr-Sauer, *English Metrical Psalms from 1600–1660* (Freiberg i. Br., 1938).

66. For a brief discussion, see Rohr-Sauer, pp. 76–79.

67. Grosart, ed., *Poems*, II: 125.

68. *Ibid.*, II: 141–42.

69. George Saintsbury, *A History of English Prosody* (New York, 1961), II: 106.

70. For brief but interesting comments by Roethke on Davies' influence on him see *On the Poet and His Craft, Selected Prose of Theodore Roethke*, ed. Ralph J. Mills, Jr. (Seattle, 1965), pp. 68–69.

Selected Bibliography

PRIMARY SOURCES

The Works in Verse and Prose of Sir John Davies. Ed. Alexander B. Grosart, Fuller Worthies Library, 3 vols. Blackburn: Printed for private circulation, 1869–1876.

The Complete Poems of Sir John Davies. Ed. Alexander B. Grosart. Early English Poets. 2 vols. London: Chatto and Windus, 1876.

The Poems of Sir John Davies. Ed. Robert Krueger. Oxford: The Clarendon Press, 1974.

The Poems of Sir John Davies. Ed. Clare Howard. New York: Columbia University Press, 1941.

Silver Poets of the Sixteenth Century. Ed. Gerald Bullett. Everyman's Library. New York: E. P. Dutton & Co., 1947.

Orchestra or a Poem of Dancing. Ed. E. M. W. Tillyard. London: Chatto & Windus, 1945.

"An Edition of *Nosce Teipsum* by Sir John Davies." Ed. Rev. T. J. Childs. Unpubl. B. Litt. thesis. Oxford University, 1939.

"The *Nosce Teipsum* of Sir John Davies: A Commentary, with Text and Introduction." Ed. Sister Mary Jerome McHale. Unpubl. doctoral diss. University of Toronto, 1942.

"An Edition of Sir John Davies' *Nosce Teipsum*." Ed. Clarence J. Simpson. Unpubl. doctoral diss. Stanford University, 1951.

"Introduction and Notes for an Edition of *Nosce Teipsum*." Ed. Ruby D. Nemser. Unpubl. doctoral diss. Harvard University, 1965.

"A Critical, Old Spelling Edition of Sir John Davies' *Nosce Teipsum*." Ed. Charles B. Taylor, Jr. Unpubl. doctoral diss. Northern Illinois University, 1971.

SECONDARY SOURCES

ANDERSON, RUTH L. *Elizabethan Psychology and Shakespeare's Plays.* University of Iowa Studies: Humanistic Series, Vol. III, No. 4. Iowa City, 1927. Useful background for the psychology presented in *Nosce Teipsum.*

BALDWIN, JOSEPH C. "John Heywood and Sir John Davies: A Change in the Tradition of the Sixteenth Century Satiric Epigram," *Satire Newsletter*, V (1967): 16–24. With Davies the satirical epigram becomes a medium of social satire.

BISHOP, C. J. "Raleigh Satirized by Harington and Davies," *Review of English Studies*, XXIII (1972): 52–56. Identifies Paulus in Davies' Epigram No. 41 with Raleigh.

BOWERS, R. H. "An Elizabethan Manuscript 'Continuation' of Sir John Davies' *Nosce Teipsum*," *Modern Philology*, LVIII (1960): 11–19. Concerns a poem by Robert Chambers entitled "A Christian Reformation of Nosce Teipsum."

BRINK, J. R. "The Composition Date of Sir John Davies' *Nosce Teipsum*," *Huntington Library Quarterly*, XXXVI (1973): 19–32. Argues that the poem was completed in manuscript by the summer of 1594.

————. "The Masque of the Nine Muses: Sir John Davies's Unpublished 'Epithalamion' and the 'Belphoebe-Ruby' Episode in *The Faerie Queene*," *Review of English Studies*, XXIII (1972): 445–47. Identifies the occasion for the poem and offers evidence that it was presented as a masque.

————. "The Rhetorical Structure of Sir John Davies's *Nosce Teipsum*," *Yearbook of English Studies*, IV (1974): 52–61. The two parts of the poem are related as question and answer and the rhetorical structure leads the reader from puzzlement to triumphant affirmation.

————. "Sir John Davies: His Life and Major Works." Unpubl. doctoral diss. Wisconsin, 1972.

BROOKE, TUCKER. "The Marlowe Canon," *PMLA* XXXVII (1922): 367–417. Discusses early printed editions of the *Epigrams*.

BUCKLEY, GEORGE T. "The Indebtedness of Sir John Davies' *Nosce Teipsum* to Philip Mornay's *Truenesse of the Christian Religion*," *Modern Philology*, XXV (1927): 67–78.

COLIE, R. L. "The Rhetoric of Transcendence," *Philological Quarterly*, XLIII (1964): 145–70. Relates *Nosce Teipsum* to other strongly Christian poems of self-knowledge by writers such as Fulke Greville, John Davies of Hereford, and John Donne.

COOPER, LANE. "Coleridge, Wordsworth, and Mr. Lowes," *PMLA* XLIII (1928): 582–92. Allusions to Davies' poetry.

CRAIK, T. W. "Volpone's Young Antinous." *Notes and Queries*, XVII (1970): 66–74. An allusion by Ben Jonson which suggests that *Orchestra* was "performed."

DOUGHTY, WILLIAM L. "The Scrutiny of the Soul, Sir John Davies—1569–1626," *Studies in the Religious Poetry of the Seventeenth Century*. London: Epworth Press, 1947. Generous appreciation of *Nosce Teipsum* and comment on John Wesley's knowledge of the work.

EBERLE, GERALD J. "Sir John Davies' *Nosce Teipsum,* 1599: a Bibliographical Puzzle," *Studies in Bibliography,* I (1948/1949): 133–48. Collation of twenty issues of the poem: discussion of the *two* editions of 1599.

ELIOT, T. S. "Sir John Davies," *On Poetry and Poets.* New York: Farrar Straus and Cudahy, 1957. Perceptive critical observations on Davies' poetry in general; *Nosce Teipsum* in particular.

FINKELPEARL, P. J. "Sir John Davies and the 'Prince d'Amour,'" *Notes and Queries,* X (1963): 300–302. Suggests Davies' attack on Richard Martin was prompted by an insult during the preceding Christmas Revels at the Temple.

––––––. *John Marston of the Middle Temple.* Cambridge: Harvard University Press, 1969. The early chapters offer an excellent discussion of the cultural life of the Inns of Court with incidental comment on Davies and other of Marston's contemporaries at the Temple.

FINNEY, GRETCHEN LUDKE. *Musical Backgrounds for English Literature: 1580–1650.* New Brunswick: Rutgers University Press, 1962. Impressive study of the symbolism of music and musical instruments in literature; incidental comment on music imagery in the *Hymnes of Astraea* and *Nosce Teipsum.*

GILL, ROMA and ROBERT KRUEGER. "The Early Editions of Marlowe's *Elegies* and Davies' *Epigrams*: Sequence and Authority," *Library,* XXVI (1971): 242–49. The relationships among the six early texts of the *Epigrams.*

HADAS, DAVID. "The Mind and Art of Sir John Davies." Unpubl. doctoral diss. Columbia, 1963.

HOLMES, MABEL DODGE. *The Poet as Philosopher.* Philadelphia: n.p., 1921. Studies three philosophical poems: *Nosce Teipsum, The Essay on Man,* and *In Memoriam.*

KRUEGER, ROBERT. "Sir John Davies: *Orchestra* Complete, *Epigrams,* Unpublished Poems," *Review of English Studies,* XIII (1962): 17–29, 113–24. A very important study. Discussion of only known manuscript text of *Orchestra* as well as other poems preserved in Bodleian Add. MS. B. 97.

LANGVARDT, ARTHUR LEROY. "The Verse Epigram in England during the Sixteenth and Early Seventeenth Centuries." Unpubl. diss. University of Colorado, 1956. Excellent study with comment (pp. 161–70) on Davies' *Epigrams.*

LIVINGSTON, JAMES L. "Sir John Davies and His *Orchestra*: Fragile

Mirror of Elizabethan Order." Unpubl. doctoral diss. Buffalo, 1970.

MEAGHER, JOHN C. "The Dance and the Masques of Ben Jonson," *Journal of the Warburg and Courtauld Institutes*, XXV (1962): 258–77. Able study of dance symbolism with brief comment on *Orchestra*.

NOSWORTHY, J. M. "The Publication of Marlowe's *Elegies* and Davies's *Epigrams*," *Review of English Studies*, IV (1953): 260–61. Suggests 1595 as date of first publication of the *Epigrams*.

PERKINSON, RICHARD H. "Additional Observations on the Later Editions of *Nosce Teipsum*," *Library*, 5th Ser., II (1947): 61–63. Bibliographical information on later editions.

—————. "The Polemical Use of Davies' *Nosce Teipsum*," *Studies in Philology*, XXXVI (1939): 597–608. Studies changes in title and in text of certain editions of the seventeenth and eighteenth centuries.

ROGERS, P. BURWELL. "Sir John Davies' Gulling *Sonnets*," *Bucknell University Studies*, IV (1954): 193–204. Best study available of these parodies.

ROHR-SAUER, PHILLIP VON. *English Metrical Psalms from 1600 to 1660. A Study in the Religions and Aesthetic Tendencies of That Period*. Freiburg: Poppem & Ortmann, 1938. Brief consideration (pp. 76–79) of Davies' translations of the Psalms.

SANDERSON, JAMES L. "Bérenger de La Tour and Sir John Davies: Two Poets Who Set the Planets Dancing," *The Library Chronicle*, XXVII (1971): 116–25. Studies the conventionality of the dance motif in *Orchestra*.

—————. "Epigrames P[er] B[enjamin] R[udyard] and Some More 'Stolen Feathers' of Henry Parrot," *Review of English Studies*, XVII (1966): 241–55. Two satiric treatments of Davies.

SEEMANN, MARGARETE. *Sir John Davies, sein Leben und seine Werke*. Vienna: Wilhelm Braumuller, 1913. Discussion in German of Davies' career, poetry, and prose.

SNEATH, E. H. *Philosophy in Poetry*. New York: Charles Scribner's Sons, 1903. Brief biography, text of *Nosce Teipsum*, and discussion of the intellectual background of the poem.

SOWTON, IAN. "Hidden Persuaders as a Means of Literary Grace," *University of Toronto Quarterly*, XXXII (1962): 55–69. Comments on instances of rhetorical forms in the "arguments" within *Orchestra*.

SPARROW, JOHN. "Some Later Editions of Sir John Davies's *Nosce*

Teipsum," *Library*, I (1946): 136–42. Comments on late seventeenth- and early eighteenth-century editions of *Nosce Teipsum*.

SPENCER, THEODORE. "Two Classic Elizabethans: Samuel Daniel and Sir John Davies" in *Theodore Spencer: Selected Essays*, ed. Alan C. Purves. New Brunswick: Rutgers University Press, 1966. Perceptive essay offering excellent critical comments on Daniel and Davies.

————. "The History of an Unfortunate Lady," *Harvard Studies and Notes in Philology and Literature*, XX (1938): 43–59. Account of the sad life and bizarre writings of Davies' wife.

TILLYARD, E. M. W. *The Elizabethan World Picture*. London: Chatto & Windus, 1943. Famous study in the history of ideas in which *Orchestra* figures for its treatment of dance as a symbol of universal order.

————. *Five Poems, 1470–1870*. London: Chatto & Windus, 1948. Includes a study of *Orchestra* as a poem reflecting the cultural and historical period of its composition.

WHIPPLE, T. K. *Martial and the English Epigram from Sir Thomas Wyatt to Ben Jonson*. Berkeley: University of California Press, 1925. Includes consideration of Davies and his adaptation of Martial's epigrams.

WILCOX, JOHN. "Informal Publication of Late Sixteenth Century Verse Satire," *Huntington Library Quarterly*, XIII (1950): 191–200. Comment on the place of satirical writing in young poets of Davies' generation.

WILKES, G. A. "The Poetry of Sir John Davies," *Huntington Library Quarterly*, XXV (1962): 283–98. Best brief study of Davies' poetry.

YATES, FRANCES. "Elizabeth as Astraea," *Journal of the Warburg and Courtauld Institutes*, X (1947): 27–82. Studies the cult and literary use of Astraea and comments on the *Hymnes of Astraea*.

Index

(The works of Davies are listed under his name)

165